THAI STYLE

THAI STYLE

Photographed by
LUCA INVERNIZZI TETTONI

Written by
WILLIAM WARREN

Edited by
GRETCHEN LIU

RIZZOLI
NEW YORK

THAI STYLE

First published in the United States of America in 1989 by
Rizzoli International Publications, Inc.
597 Fifth Avenue, New York, NY   10017

Copyright ©   TIMES EDITIONS
                 1 New Industrial Road, Singapore 1953.

Library of Congress Cataloging-in-Publication Data

Warren, William.
    Thai style/William Warren; photographs by Luca Invernizzi
Tettoni.
       p.   cm.
    ISBN 0-8478-1043-7
    1. Interior decoration – Thailand.   I. Invernizzi, Luca.
II. Title.
NK2078.7.A1W37   1989   88-43422
747.29593 – dc19   CIP

Printed and bound in Singapore

ACKNOWLEDGEMENTS

This book would not have been possible without the generous assistance of many people, to whom the author and photographer are deeply indebted.

We would particularly like to thank our consultants, Khun Chaiwut Tulayadhan of Neold and Khun Chantaka Puranananda of Pure Design, who introduced us to many homes we would not otherwise have discovered, lent items from their collections to be photographed, and devoted many valuable hours of their time to the project.

Dr. Chalermsri Jan-Orn of Chulalongkorn University assisted in the research and provided translations of Thai source material on traditional Thai architecture. Khun Kiatikul Tiyanukulmongkol is responsible for most of the architectural drawings of buildings and details.

Our gratitude also goes to Mrs. Banyen Aksonsri of the Banyen Folk Art Museum in Chiang Mai, Khun Chalie Amatyakul of the Oriental Hotel, Dr. Hans G. Banziger, Mr. James Bastable, His Excellency Ivan Bastouil the French Ambassador to Thailand, Mr. and Mrs. Diether Von Boehm-Bezing, Mr. William Booth, Khun Tula and Khun Chancham Bunnag, Mr. and Mrs. Jean-Michel Beurdeley, Acharn Ruthai Chaichongrak, Khun Manop Charoensuk, Mr. Achille Clarac and Mr. Henri Pagau-Clarac, Mrs. Joanna Cross, M.L. Tridhosyuth Devakul, Mr. Donald Gibson and Khun Duangkamol Srisuksri of the Mengrai Kilns in Chiang Mai, His Excellency Jose de Mello Gouveia the Portuguese Ambassador to Thailand, Mr. Dennis Grace, Mrs. Marsha Ginthin-Jones, Dr. Pongsri Lekwatana, Khunying Wualai Leelanuch, Mr. and Mrs. Timothy Lewis, Khun Pornsri Luphaiboon of the Oriental Hotel, Mr. Islay Lyons, Mrs. Connie Mangskau, Mrs. Laiad Meier, Mr. and Mrs. Karl Morsbach, Khun Surat Osthanugrah, Mr. Gerald Pierce, Khun S. Reuycharoeng, Mr. William Riley, Khunying Lurasakdi and Khun Phinit Sampatisiri, Khun Uab Sanasen, Khun Pornchai Suchitta of the Siam Society, Mr. and Mrs. Tom Tofield, Pol. Lt. Col. Sprung and Khun Anong Ulapathorn, Khun Marisa Viravaidhya, Khun Venica Vil, Mr. Ian White, and the National Museum of Lopburi.

Last, but by no means least, we would like to thank Mrs. Gretchen Liu, who has provided invaluable support throughout the project with her editorial skills and wise counsel.

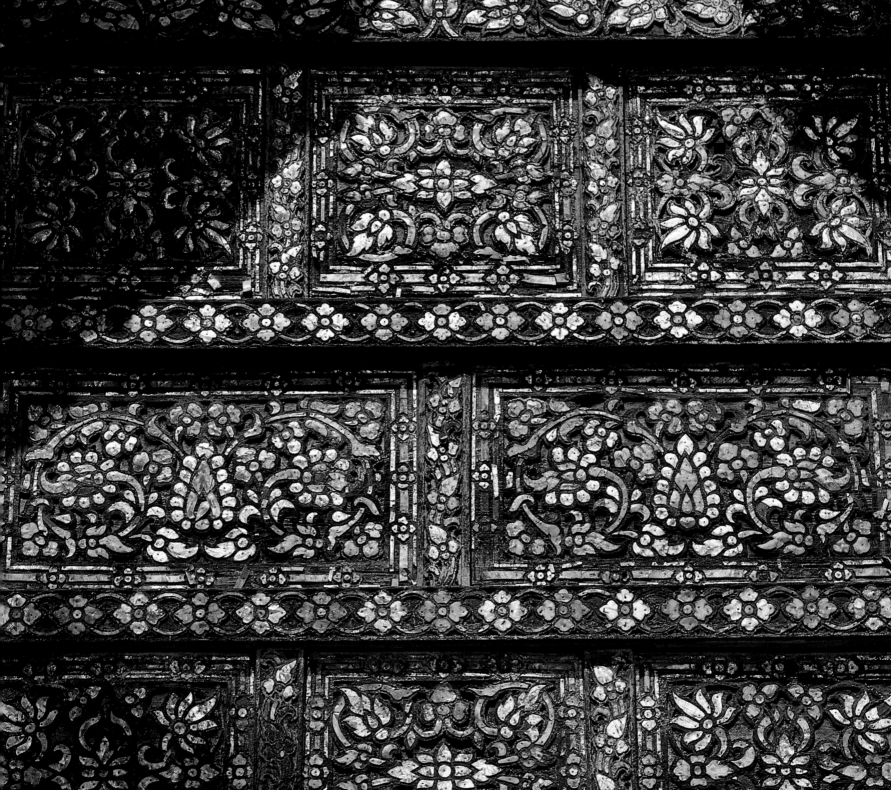

CONTENTS

INTRODUCTION

The special style that defines a culture is born of many elements. Thai style, so vividly revealed in its art and architecture, is the product of its distinctive landscape, its skillful use of varied influences, and a history unique among the nations of Southeast Asia.

Thailand today is a multi-faceted kingdom of 50 million people, most of them Thai in the ethnic sense but many of them Chinese, Malay, Indian, Khmer, and other races who have played important cultural roles. It is also a kingdom of contrasts: new and old styles coexisting, now and then subtly merging in ways that often enchant, sometimes surprise, and occasionally bewilder an outsider.

Buddhist temples encrusted with ornate decorations, baroque fantasies at once witty and other-worldly, rise on crowded city streets, and during lulls in the traffic din you can hear the faint music of bells and the soothing sound of monks chanting. Along rivers and canals, motor boats speed past plain but striking traditional houses, their graceful peaked roofs silhouetted against the pale tropic sky. In the market places of the far north, amid tape recorders, plastic pails, and other artifacts of the modern world, you will find tribal people in bizarre costumes of medieval splendor. The King of Thailand now lives in a wholly Western palace, adorned with the communications antennae through which he keeps in touch with his farflung projects around the country, but within the same compound reside the royal white elephants,

A lacquer cabinet of the Ayutthaya period, now displayed in the National Library and regarded as one of the finest examples of Ayutthayan craftsmanship. The detail shown represents a stem of rice with various animals and symbolizes the abundance of the Thai countryside. PREVIOUS PAGE: *Detail from the gable of Wat Phra That Luang in northern Thailand.*

A chedi at Sukhothai, the first Thai capital between the 13th and 15th centuries.

treasured symbols of monarchy since the first rulers began to shape a national identity.

Uniting these disparate elements like a slender but surprisingly tough thread is a spirit unmistakably Thai. To fully appreciate it, to comprehend the complex creation of "Thai Style" it is necessary to go back to the kingdom's earliest days.

About a thousand years ago, in the opinion of most scholars, the first sizeable groups of Thais began to migrate southward from the Chinese province of Yunnan to the region they would make their home. They came seeking greater independence for the distinctive culture they had developed over many centuries, and they came, too, like most of the world's migrant peoples, in search of better land and room for expansion. They were to be notably successful in both quests.

The country now known as Thailand offered the newcomers wide topographical variety and a wealth of natural resources. The mountainous north was rich in hard-wood timber trees, an easily available source of building material, and watered by numerous streams and rivers. The far south, a narrow isthmus stretching like a long finger to the Malay states, enjoyed a plentiful supply of seafood from the seas off its two coastlines, as well as rare ores and precious stones. The northeastern plateau, semi-arid today, was then thickly forested and amply supplied with water. Most alluring of all was the Chao Phya River basin, a self-contained geopolitical unit and one of the world's most fertile rice-producing areas, where most of the great Thai kingdoms were to rise in future centuries.

Earlier groups were also drawn to these riches. Archaeologists have found evidence of prehistoric settlers going back to the Paleolithic Age, 500,000 years ago, in places as widely separated as Chiang Rai in the north and Kanchanaburi west of Bangkok. The most significant development occurred on the Khorat Plateau in the northeast, where, beginning around 4,000 B.C., a remarkable culture rose and flourished until shortly after the beginning of the Christian era. Known as Ban Chiang, after the small village where the first discoveries were made, its people cultivated rice, wove textiles, and made pottery decorated with stylish red geometric designs; particularly intriguing to historians is the fact that by around 3000 B.C. — far earlier than any previous estimates, perhaps as early as anywhere — they had learned to produce some of the world's first bronze and copper tools, which later developed into highly sophisticated items of daily use and personal adornment.

Pending further discoveries, an aura of mystery still clings to the people of Ban Chiang and their subsequent fate. Did their methods of clearing land lead to its impoverishment, driving them down from the plateau? Did they pass on any of their skills to later inhabitants? The answers are a matter of conjecture; all we know is that their culture came to

Spires and rooftops of the Grand Palace and Temple of the Emerald Buddha in Bangkok.

an end around 200 A.D., and about the same time other performers appeared on the stage of history.

Two of the most important were the Mons and the Khmers, both of whom had considerable influence on the development of Thai culture. The former, establishing a kingdom known as Dvaravati, settled in the western half the Chao Phya River valley, while the latter made their home on part of the northeast plateau and in modern Cambodia. Buddhism was introduced from India, according to legend, around the third century B.C. by missionaries of the Emperor Asoke, and Indian influence remained strong for several centuries, especially on Buddhist art in the south of the country.

By the 12th century A.D. the Khmers were the most powerful group, ruling from the mighty temple city of Angkor. Their empire covered much of present-day Thailand, and the remains of their *prang*-centered temples, rich in Hindu symbolism, can be found scattered through the northeast and in the central plains as well. But Khmer power was weakening, and the time was ripe for later arrivals to assert themselves and create a style of their own.

The first Thais formed city-states in various parts of the far north, in places like Chiang Saen, Chiang Rai, and Chiang Mai, united for a time in a loose federation known as Lanna Thai but never exerting much power outside the region. Other groups left the mountains, however, and by the 13th century there were substantial Thai populations in the plains below and even — somewhat mysteriously — as far south as Nakorn Sri Thammarat. At Sukhothai, near the northern edge of the plains, they probably outnumbered the Khmer overlords, and around 1243 three of their chieftans united to establish the first truly independent Thai kingdom.

Sukhothai lasted less than 200 years, but during that time it was the scene of extraordinary cultural achievements, among them the evolution of Thai concepts of kingship, the invention of Thai writing, and the beginnings of Thai styles of art and architecture. Its prosperity and freedom from unfair constraints is celebrated in a famous inscription dating from 1292 during the reign of King Ram-khamhaeng, still learned by every Thai schoolchild: "There is fish in the water and rice in the fields. The lord of the realm does not levy a toll on his subjects for travelling the roads, they lead their cattle to trade or their horses to sell, whoever wants to trade in elephants, does so; whoever wants to trade in horses, does so; whoever wants to trade in silver or gold, does so."

Sukhothai today is filled with hundreds of ruins, all of them religious buildings. These monasteries, or *wats*, reflect borrowings from a wide variety cultures, principally Khmer, Mon, and Singhalese, but they also display a number of uniquely Thai features like the graceful lotus-bud tower that became the spiritual

Traditional Thai houses, in the style characteristic of the Central Plains region.

symbol of the kingdom and highly original images of the Buddha in bronze and stucco relief. Chinese potters, supposedly brought by King Ramkhamhaeng, introduced the art of making fine ceramics and Sukhothai wares were exported in large quantities to Indonesia, Borneo and the Philippines.

Due to a custom which forbade the use of durable materials like brick and stone for any but religious buildings, nothing remains of Sukhothai's palaces or domestic houses, all of which were built of wood or bamboo. From fragmentary mural paintings that survive in temples of the north, however, it seems probable that the houses were simple structures with steep thatched roofs, raised off the ground to afford protection from floods and wild animals, and displaying few if any non-functional decorations. The palaces were larger, to judge from the area they occupied, and may have been adorned with woodcarvings appropriate to their royal residents, but again were basically plain with unpainted wooden walls hung on a frame of stout poles.

Thai architecture evolved further in Ayutthaya, a new kingdom that arose in the Chao Phya basin during the 14th century, and so did the fortunes of the Thai people. From a small town with rough mud fortifications, Ayutthaya grew in both size and splendor until by the late 17th century it had a population of more than a million and a skyline of flashing temple spires and elegant multi-tiered roofs overlooking miles of crowded waterways lined with houses.

Sukhothai wats had been relatively subdued except for their stucco decorations; by contrast, those of Ayutthaya at its peak were magnificent with gold leaf, colored tile mosaics, elaborately carved wooden gables, vast murals, and doors ornamented with delicate gold-and-black lacquer paintings, incorporating designs often borrowed from Khmer or Indian sources but given a particular flavor that turned them into something Thai. Since its rulers adopted the Khmer concept of divine kingship, palaces underwent a similar transformation and many features of the temples appeared in their decoration; starting in the reign of King Narai (1657-1688), they were also made from brick, adding to their imposing appearance. The first Western-style buildings appeared in the Ayutthaya period as well, one of them a palace with European decorations in the summer capital of Lopburi, where a French embassy was received by Narai.

Domestic houses, of course, were simpler but apparently had the airy raised platforms and practical construction that we know today. Simon de la Loubère, who came in Narai's reign, described the majority as being made of bamboo and unusually portable: when three houses happened to block the king's view of a proposed firearms demonstration, "the proprietors had taken and carried them away with their furniture in less than an hour."

Bangkok, established as the seat of government by

*Evening view of Chiang Mai, once the capital of an
independent northern kingdom.*

King Rama I in 1782, was originally modelled after Ayutthaya, totally destroyed by the Burmese 15 years before. In its first 50 years or so, it was almost wholly Thai in appearance, a conscious effort to reproduce the glories of the old capital through general layout and specific buildings. Early travellers commented on its splendid wats, its mile-square Grand Palace compound, the densely-packed double rows of floating shops that lined the Chao Phya, and the network of Venice-like canals that served as streets.

The evolution of the central Thai domestic house, with its distinctive curved roofends and paneled walls, was now complete, and hundreds of them could be seen throughout the city, some of impressive size and workmanship while others were simple in the extreme. Joseph Conrad, who came as a sailor in the late 19th century, described "an expanse of brown houses of bamboo, mats, of leaves, of a vegetable-matter style of architecture, sprung out of the brown soil on the banks of the muddy river. It was amazing to think that in those miles of human habitation there was not probably half a dozen pounds of nails."

But even when Conrad wrote, this water-oriented phase of Bangkok's history was drawing to a close, doomed by the rapid growth of its population and new concepts of urban life. Alone among the countries of the region Thailand never had an alien culture imposed on it through European colonization. Nevertheless, Western influence penetrated with increas-

ing force, making itself felt first in the capital and then, at a somewhat more gradual pace, on more remote parts of the kingdom.

Roads appeared and with them shops and houses of solid construction, in foreign styles. As the canals lost their vital importance as arteries of communication, more and more of them were allowed to silt up and eventually became streets to accommodate the growing number of vehicles. Much of what remained of the distant exotic past either vanished during the building boom that started soon after the second world war or retreated to seldom-seen byways, hidden in the shadows of a brand-new skyline. The transformation was so great, both in the city and outside, that a casual visitor today may find it difficult to find the elements that were once so distinctive.

Closer inspection, however, reveals the tenacious strength of Thai style. In its purest forms it survives through the fanciful temples and the more subdued yet elegant classic houses, both of which continue to be built. It can be found as well in many structures that remain from the later 19th and early 20th centuries — more than may appear at first glance — outwardly so foreign in appearance yet still responding to landscape, climate, and social demands in a peculiarly Thai way. Finally, it is present in numerous contemporary homes, in which traditional concepts and modern building materials are combined to create new versions of Thai style.

SUKOTHAI

Sukhothai, where the Thais established their first capital, ruled for less than two centuries, between 1238 and 1368, yet was the scene of remarkable developments both political and cultural. The Thai alphabet was devised here, as well as many distinctively Thai ornamental and architectural features. Among the latter was the graceful lotus-bud finial seen on the right on a *chedi* at Wat Mahathat, the largest of the numerous ruined religious buildings that still stand in the old city. No trace remains of Sukhothai's domestic houses and palaces, which were constructed of wood or bamboo.

AYUTTHAYA

Ayutthaya, which overpowered Sukhothai in the 14th century, was the capital of the kingdom for nearly 400 years. At its peak, in the 17th century, it was filled with magnificent palaces and temples and had a population estimated at more than a million, larger than London at the time, among them many foreign traders. The city fell to the Burmese in 1767, after which most of its treasures were looted or destroyed by fire. The large temple shown on the left is Wat Phra Ram, founded in 1369 but completely restored in 1741.

RURAL AND URBAN

For much of Thailand's history, and in rural areas today as well, water has been the dominant natural feature of life, nourishing the essential rice fields and providing an important means of communication. In the central plains the principal artery is the Chao Phya River, and on its fertile banks have risen three capitals — Ayutthaya, Dhonburi, and Bangkok — along with countless smaller communities. Canals stretch far into the countryside and serve as roads linking various villages.

With more than six million people, Bangkok today (following pages), is some 45 times the size of the next largest city in Thailand. In its early days, life was centered on the river, overlooked by the mile-square Grand Palace and also by most of the foreign legations and commercial establishments. Toward the end of the 19th century, the city began to move away from the Chao Phya, across miles of former rice fields, eventually acquiring a modern skyline of towering office buildings to replace the old exotic one of gilded temple spires.

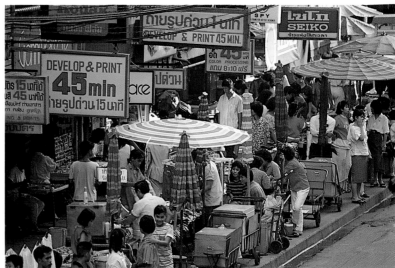

THAI FORMS

The sinuous elegance of curves, contrasting with the formality of rigid geometric patterns; an occasional sense of grave restraint, almost but not quite amounting to severity, relieved by moments of exhilarating artistic abandon; now and then a sudden touch of pure whimsy, sometimes expressed through bold colors, sometimes through odd forms, so unexpected and lighthearted it brings an involuntary smile of delight.

Recognition of Thai style is easier than analysis; its varied components tend to be elusive, like the hot, sweet, and sour flavors of the country's food, each making its presence felt but in ways so subtle that it is difficult to say where one stops and another begins.

At every turn, though, the eye is constantly discovering memorable manifestations of the phenomenon in creations large and small, humble and exalted: the slender, refined finials known as *chofahs*, or "bunch of sky," that grace temple roofs and provide a note of fantasy; the abstract patterns formed by both brightly-hued tiles and simple thatch; the intricate mother-of-pearl designs embedded in a lacquered door or a betel-nut box; the sense of color and pattern that transforms floral decorations into minor works of art; the simplest of traditional household utensils, fish traps and rice baskets, water jars and coconut scrapers, in which function is combined with an innate beauty of form; even the primitive artwork that adorns modern vehicles.

Detail from the top of an ecclesiastical chair in Wat Phratat Lampang Luang near Lampang in the north, donated by the Prince of Lampang to the temple in 1855; wood, lacquered and gilded, with inlaid glass mosaic. The chair is approximately 2.3 m high, the detail shown here about life size.

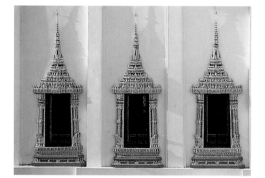

EARLY BANGKOK

Multi-tiered roofs are the most memorable feature of Thai temple and palace architecture and dominate the landscape. The first royal buildings in Bangkok, founded as the capital in 1782, were conscious evocations of those that lay in ruins in Ayutthaya. Of particular splendor was the mile-square Grand Palace on the Chao Phya River, which contains some of the finest examples of traditional Thai art and architecture.

ABOVE: *Windows with gilded stucco decorations on the Dusit Maha Prasat in the Grand Palace, dating from the reign of King Rama I (1782-1809).*
RIGHT: *Tiered roofs and gilt-mosaic finials known as* chofas *on the Amarindra Vinitchai Audience Hall, built by King Rama I in the palace compound at the beginning of the Bangkok period.*

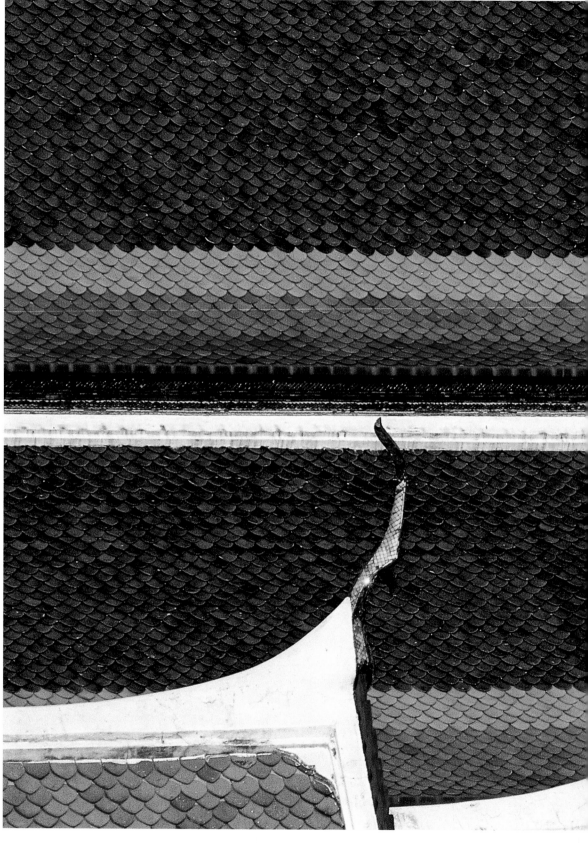

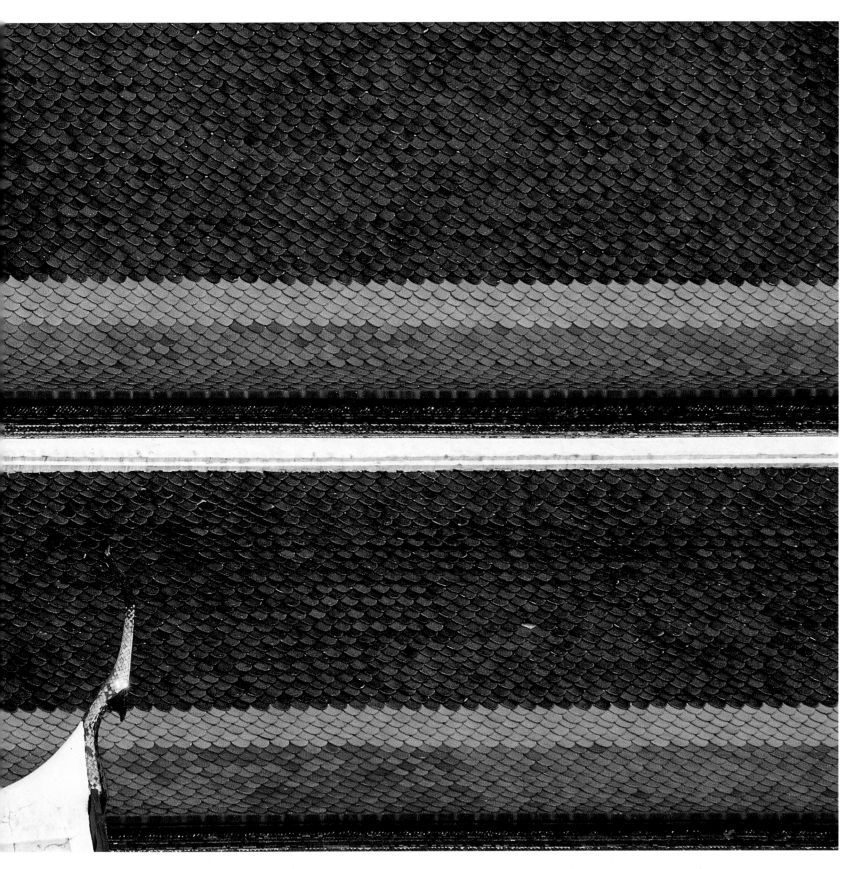

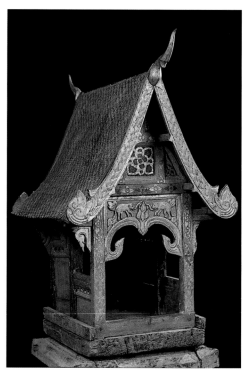

LANNA THAI AND AYUTTHAYA

The earliest Thai city states were established in the north, in a loose federation called Lanna Thai. During the Ayutthaya Period (1350-1767) Thai style reached a peak of elegant craftsmanship in many parts of the kingdom.

ABOVE: *Model of a temple in Lanna Thai style, 19th century; painted wood with glass inlays, approximately 80 cm high (Banyen Folk Art Museum, Chiang Mai).*
LEFT: *Window of the* vihan, *or assembly hall, at Wat Phantao in Chiang Mai, early 19th century. The Makara arch above the window is gilded woodcarving with inlaid mosaic, and the motif, also found at Sukhothai, is of Indonesian (Srivijaya) origin; the barred window shows Khmer influence.*

BELOW: *Model of an Ayutthayan* vihan, *18th century; wood, painted and gilded, height approximately 60 cm. The model clearly shows certain features of Ayutthayan architecture such as the boat-shaped podium, called a* thawng-samphao *(ship's hull), and tiered roofs (Wat Machimawat Museum, Songkla).*

RIGHT: *Window of the library at Wat Saket in Bangkok, in the same shape as the windows on the model* vihan, *wood with gold-and-black lacquer decoration; each panel about 130 cm high and 30 cm wide. The library was moved to Wat Saket from Ayutthaya by King Rama I (1782-1809) and probably dates from the late 17th or early 18th century. The panel decorations show foreign merchants, a theme that originated in 17th-century Ayutthaya and persisted until the early Bangkok (Ratanakosin) period; the window frame is decorated with finely-carved Chinese dragons and inlaid mosaics, while the library walls are lacquered wood with Sino-Thai motifs.*

DECORATIVE ARTS

Wood and stucco, glass mosaics, patterned textiles, gleaming lacquer covered with delicate paintings in gold: these were some of the mediums through which the traditional Thai artisan expressed his imagination. Motifs recurred over the centuries, sometimes with subtle variations, always with an exuberant sense of color and an eye for detail. Similar designs, for instance, are found in both Ayutthayan and early Rattanakosin (Bangkok) decoration, though in the latter they have become far more profuse, usually covering every part of a surface in rich but somewhat rigid geometric patterns.

LEFT: *Painting of guardian divinities on the interior of doors at Wat Yai Suwannaram in Petchaburi, late 17th or early 18th century.*
RIGHT: *Thai ornamentation, as seen in different mediums: (Top left) Glass mosaic at Phra Phutthabat in Saraburi; (Top right) Glazed tiles and stucco at Wat Rajabopitr in Bangkok; (Middle, right and left) Textiles printed with Thai designs in India in the early 19th century; (Bottom left) Gilded woodcarving at Wat Rajabopitr in Bangkok; (Bottom right) Detail from a scripture cabinet decorated with gold and black lacquer, early Bangkok period, in the National Museum.*

THAI POTTERY

The earliest pottery found in Thailand dates from prehistoric times. During the Sukhothai period (13th-14th centuries) beautiful glazed wares with distinctive Thai designs were made and exported to several countries in the region; Ayutthaya (1350-1767) produced only unglazed pottery, though large quantities of porcelain were imported from China.

ABOVE: *Glazed stoneware with fish designs, produced in Sukhothai kilns in the 14th century; diameter of the plate on the left is 23.5 cm.*
LEFT: *Fish plate with border motif of creeping plants; diameter 31 cm (Surat Osathanugrah Collection).*

ABOVE LEFT: *Water jar with lid and stand in baked clay, from the late Ayutthaya period; height of the jar 50 cm (Neold Collection).*
ABOVE RIGHT: *Unglazed stoneware jar from a kiln at Si Satchanalai near Sukhothai (Surat Osathanugrah Collection).*
LEFT: *Pottery with red-on-buff designs found at Ban Chiang in northeastern Thailand; these date from the later period of Ban Chiang, between 300 B.C. and 200 A.D. The tallest pot is about 45 cm tall, the pedestalled pot about 22 cm (Suan Pakkad Palace Collection).*

FURNITURE

Traditional Thai homes, particularly of the lower classes, contained relatively little furniture beyond a few storage containers and woven reed mats for sleeping. More elaborate pieces were found in palaces and in houses belonging to wealthier members of society, as well as in Buddhist temples where the scripture cabinets and ecclesiastical chairs were often works of high art that employed such skills as woodcarving, lacquer, and inlaid glass mosaics. With increasing Western influence, European furniture began to appear, sometimes decorated with Thai motifs, sometimes adapted to Thai customs, as in the case of low dressing tables.

LEFT: *Three decorative details from traditional Thai furniture. The one at the top, from a library cabinet in the Lopburi Museum, includes angels probably inspired by European influence in the late 17th century. In the middle detail, from an early Ratanakosin period bed, similar figures have become characters from Thai mythology. Below is a part of a Thai table in the collection of Khun Chaiwut Tulayadhan.*

ABOVE LEFT: *A chair with legs in the shape of elephant heads and trunks (Banyen Folk Art Museum Collection).*
ABOVE RIGHT: *A 19th-century Thai dressing table (Neold Collection).*
LEFT: *A traditional seat for monks (Neold Collection).*

ELEGANT RATANAKOSIN UTENSILS

The first half of the Ratanakosin Period, as the Bangkok era is called in Thai, saw a continuation of the love of color and intricate decoration that had characterized Ayutthaya. Artisans, often under royal patronage, produced a wide range of fine traditional crafts for use in palaces and aristocratic homes; other items were produced abroad with the designs being supplied from Thailand.

LEFT: *Silver holder, with glasses and decanter imported from Europe.*
ABOVE: *A Thai lacquer tray, inlaid with mother-of-pearl patterns, holds a collection of crystal bowls made in Europe to Thai designs during the reign of King Rama V.*
TOP RIGHT: *Enamel teapot, with traditional Thai design, from Nakorn Sri Thammarat.*
TOP FAR RIGHT AND BOTTOM RIGHT: *Examples of Bencharong, a pentachromatic ware made in China for export to Thailand with Thai patterns, which first appeared in the latter part of the Ayutthaya period and continued to be produced throughout most of the 19th century.*
BOTTOM FAR RIGHT: *A betel box set in nielloware, a craft for which Nakorn Sri Thammarat is still celebrated.*

FURNISHINGS OF
A NORTHERN HOUSEHOLD

Plentiful natural resources, together with a variety of artisan communities, have traditionally made northern Thailand a center of such crafts as woodcarving, lacquerware, silver, ceramics, and ivory work. In Chiang Mai, separate villages, each specializing in a particular art, once stood just outside the city walls; today they have been absorbed into the urban area, yet even so craftsmen tend to group in the old areas and pass down skills from generation to generation.

ABOVE: *An assortment of red and black lacquer boxes, used for keeping betel (Neold Collection).*

RIGHT: *At top are a wooden betel box and a group of lacquerware items that includes a* kantoke *tray used in northern dinners, a water jar, and a glutinous rice basket (Banyen Folk Art Museum Collection). In the middle are silver betel containers in a red and black lacquer box (Banyen Folk Art Museum) and a selection of northern ceramics. At bottom are ceremonial knives (Banyen Folk Art Museum) and samples of decorated lacquerware (Neold).*

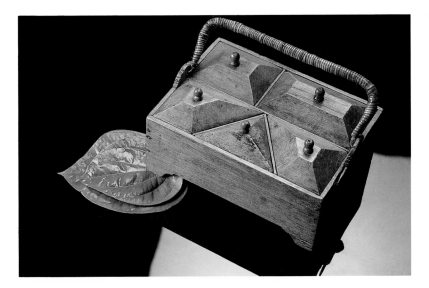

EVERYDAY UTENSILS OF RURAL LIFE

Following techniques and designs handed down for generations, and utilizing easily available local materials, Thai villages still make most of the goods needed in their daily life. As in the past, these simple items not only serve a specific purpose but also often display a striking elegance of form.

ABOVE: *A typical* lan kruang jak san, *as shops selling kitchen utensils and other household goods are known, in Nakorn Phanom near the Laotian border.*

RIGHT: *A selection of the items used in daily life in rural Thailand, all handmade from local materials: (1) hats from the north, (2) a ladle made from a coconut, (3) a basket for carrying a chicken in Chiang Mai, (4) rice baskets, (5) water bottles made from gourds, (6) brooms, (7) a container for keeping freshly-caught fish, found throughout the country, (8) northern containers for glutinous rice, (9) a container for rice.*

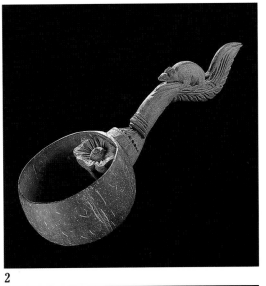

1

2

3

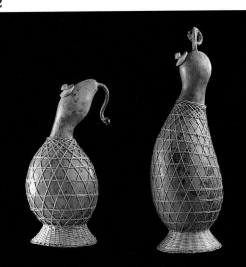

4

5

6

7

8

9

CONTINUING CRAFTS

Most of Thailand's traditional crafts continue to be produced in various parts of the country, stimulated in recent years by a new appreciation of their beauty and utility.

ABOVE: *Contemporary celadon wares produced by the Mengrai Kilns in Chiang Mai, where the ancient art of fine ceramics, started in the Sukhothai period, still survives.*
RIGHT: *In the two pictures at top, workers at the Mengrai Kilns are shown placing wares in the biscuit (moderate heat) kiln and applying chisled decorations to pots. The other pictures show the dyeing, preparation, and weaving of indigo ikat cloth in the northeast, the traditional center of weaving in Thailand; the pattern shown on the cloth is typical of those produced in the region.*

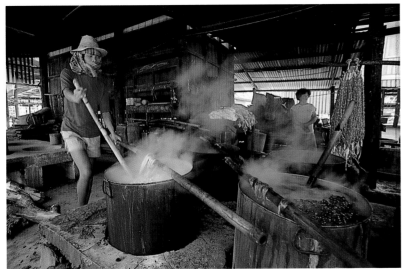

STREET ART

Mythology as well as the Thai love of color distinguishes many of the decorations that adorn otherwise mundane trucks, taxis, buses, and motor tricycles on city streets as well as on boats and buffalo carts. Among the legendary creatures shown on these pages — all of which can be found in traditional temple mural paintings as well — are voluptuous mermaids, mythical lions, dragons, and the half-human half-bird *kinaree*. Such decorations originally served as magic protection and in many cases still do.

SPIRITUAL ABODES

A feature of every Thai compound is a small structure, usually elevated on a pole, to house the spiritual guardian of the property (following pages); these are often simple wooden replicas of the traditional domestic dwelling but may also be elaborate affairs of colored cement modeled after religious buildings. Other spirit houses are placed near sacred trees, in caves, and at a particularly dangerous place on a road. All are kept supplied with regular offerings of incense, flowers, and food, as well as doll-like figures that represent spiritual attendants.

LEFT: *Design on a boat in Narathiwat.*
RIGHT: *Designs on vehicles in Bangkok.*

TRADITIONS

In the first decade of the present century, an English painter named P.A. Thompson passed a pleasant day touring Bangkok by boat, then still the most convenient way to explore Thailand's capital. On one suburban *klong*, or canal, he came across a number of houses "of the typical, low-country type," which he described as follows:

A platform of teak planks is supported on piles, six or seven feet above the level of the ground, and approached by a ladder leading down into the klong. *Opening on to two sides of the platform are little houses, also built of teak, with graceful gable ends curving upward to a sharp point. In the city the roofs are tiled, but here they are generally thatched with attap. If the people are very poor, perhaps they will only have a platform of bamboos, and the walls of the house will also be of split bamboo and attap interlaced. The platform is often gay with flowering shrubs, amongst which brilliant butterflies flit about. It forms the courtyard, from which it is only a step up to the floors of the houses. The sleeping-rooms are at the back, but in front and open to the platform are deep verandahs, in which the family live during the day.*

Every foreign visitor to Bangkok who put his thoughts to paper commented in awe, and often at considerable length, on the city's dazzling Buddhist temples, which reveal Thai style at its most ornate.

A ngao, *the decorative feature at the end of the bargeboard on most traditional Thai houses. Experts differ in their interpretation of these ornamental flourishes, which are found in a wide range of shapes both simple and complex.*

47

Detail of an 11th-century stone-carving on a Khmer temple in northeastern Thailand with carved decorations at the roof-ends.

Somerset Maugham's reaction was characteristic:

They are gorgeous; they glitter with gold and whitewash, yet are not garish; against that vivid sky, in that dazzling sunlight, they hold their own, defying the brilliancy of nature and supplementing it with the ingenuity and playful boldness of man. The artists who developed them step by step from the buildings of the ancient Khmers had the courage to pursue their fantasy to the limit; I fancy that art meant little to them, they desired to express a symbol; they knew no reticence, they cared nothing for good taste; and if they achieved art it is as men achieve happiness, not by pursuing it, but by doing with all their heart whatever in the day's work needs doing.

Most travellers also found space for a description of the impressive double rows of floating shophouses that lined the Chao Phya River and reminded them of an Asian Venice. Thompson, however, is one of the few to dwell in any detail on the classic domestic Thai house — less spectacular than the religious buildings, to be sure, but nevertheless a remarkable architectural achievement in its own right, displaying a style both practical and uniquely Thai.

The structure Thompson admired, with its steep roof, its spare but elegant decorative features, its prefabricated paneled walls, and its rooms opening on to a breezy upper platform, was the Central Thai house, probably the best known of at least three distinct styles in various parts of the country. Whether all have evolved from a common origin is a matter of scholarly debate: some of the leading experts on the subject believe each developed independently out of different influences, despite similarities in construction. Others, who favor the evolutionary theory, point to the existence of certain architectural features on houses and Buddhist temples in the southernmost provinces of China, where large communities of ethnic Thais still live.

Though summers are humid, winter temperatures drop to freezing in this part of China, and the houses are designed for warmth. Those of the ethnic Thai are raised from the ground and made of wood or bamboo, with steep roofs that are thatched or tiled. The more permanent wooden ones usually consist of a large room with only a few small windows for air circulation. A single stove placed near the entrance serves for both heating the house and cooking, and mats for sleeping are arranged near the source of warmth. Trapped by the lack of ventilation, the smoke has stained the unpainted walls black, and the atmosphere is generally dark and faintly claustrophobic, almost the opposite of the popular conception of a Thai house elsewhere.

What identifies the structures as Thai, and distinguishes them from Chinese houses in the area, is the elevation from the ground, even though in some

Detail from a mural painting at Wat Phra Singh in Chiang Mai; the roof-end decorations are similar to those seen on the Khmer temple on the facing page.

cases it may be less than a meter, and the steep roofs, sometimes multi-layered, with expansive overhangs to protect the interior from both rain and sun. Some of the bamboo houses, in fact, are raised quite high, with the open air platform outside the sleeping room that is such a notable feature of traditional houses in Thailand itself.

Homes in the northern part of the present-day country were once probably similar to these, since winters there a thousand years ago, when the Thais began to drift down, were as cold as in China. Deforestation, rapidly increasing as more and more settlers arrived, led to warmer weather for much of the year, and homes 'changed accordingly, acquiring characteristics of the style now known as Lanna Thai. Stoves, used for cooking rather than for heating, were moved outside the sleeping quarters into a separate kitchen, often some distance away, and there were more and larger windows. As ventilation became an important consideration, the elevation of the house from the ground increased, creating a convenient open space below which could be used to keep domestic animals or for such activities as cloth-weaving and woodcarving.

The best-known northern-style dwelling today is the one popularly called a "*kalae* house," the name being derived from a prominent V-shaped design formed by extending the roof supports beyond the ridge-pole on both ends of the structure. "*Kalae*" has

been variously translated as "glancing crows" and "glancing pigeons," and some authorities believe one of its non-structural purposes may have been to discourage crows and other large birds from lighting on the roof. Others think the feature symbolizes a pair of horns, citing the fact that in ancient times buffalo horns were often placed on roof-tops to show the wealth of the family. A number of studies are currently being made on the subject but thus far the answer remains a matter of conjecture.

On the simplest houses, especially those made of bamboo, the *kalae* are nothing more than rather crude extensions, possibly serving a functional purpose by simplifying construction and further strengthening the roof. On a house belonging to a more prosperous family, however, they are often separate pieces, beautifully carved in a shape that does indeed suggest feathers, or perhaps flickering flames, and that provides a decorative effect not unlike the curved finials at either end of Thai temple roofs. *Kalae* are also found on houses of some of the hill tribes who live in the northern mountains, as well as those of the Thai Lu people in southern China and Laos; they are rarely seen on houses in central and southern Thailand.

The classic northern house, rectangular in shape, is raised a considerable distance off the ground on sturdy round posts, oriented north and south to expose it to the prevailing winds. Wood is used

throughout, and the walls, doors, windows, and gable ends are made as separate units, an early form of prefabrication that was being practiced in Thailand centuries before its advantages were recognized by Western architects. Using joints of wood held in place by wooden pegs — never nails in the older houses — the components are then hung on the pillars, the walls slanting outward from the floor to the lower edge of the roof, which is either tiled, wood-shingled or thatched according to the fortunes of the owner. The outward-leaning walls are one of the marks that distinguish the northern house from that of the central plains, in which both the pillars and the walls incline slightly inward toward the top, adding to its graceful suggestion of height.

Because teak was the most abundant building material in the northern hills, it was the wood favored for construction of the better houses, both in the north and in the central region. The pillars supporting the house, however, were traditionally of stronger wood, usually a pair of each variety. Certain woods were taboo, however, because their names in Thai had inauspicious associations; one, for instance, sounded like the word for "corpse," while another, the *yon* tree, was never used because it was believed that it harbored spirits who might bring trouble to the residents. As we shall see later, similar beliefs come into play in the selection of plants for a Thai garden.

At the foot of the stairs leading to the upper platform, a trough of water is placed for washing the feet, since no shoes are worn above — a custom that

Detail of a mural in Wat Mongkut in Bangkok, showing an improvised showerbath.

has given rise to a northern saying that a wet lower step is a happy sign since it suggests the family is honored by many visitors. Hospitable households in the region also often place an earthernware jar of cool water just outside the gate for the benefit of thirsty strangers who might pass by.

The smallest house consists of a covered but otherwise open verandah, slightly raised above the level of the upper platform, and behind it a large room that serves as the family sleeping quarters. Windows in the sleeping room are often small, perhaps a legacy of the distant past, though it is likely to be cool thanks to the high roof and absence of a ceiling. The kitchen is separate, either a small room or a covered area on the platform. In large families, this basic plan may be elaborated so that two or more rooms, each an individual structure, are built on the platform. Eating and other family activities take place on the verandah, which also serves as a sleeping place for younger male members and male guests.

Aside from the *kalae* and the outward leaning walls, the classic northern-style house has another feature that distinguishes it from houses of central Thailand. The inner room, where the owner and his wife sleep, is believed to contain not only the ancestral spirits but also the virility and fertility of the couple who lives there. Above the doors leading to it are placed carved wooden lintels known as *ham yon*, which in the old language of the north can be

translated as "magic testicles," and these both preserve the strength of the family and protect it from outside evils.

A Chiang Mai scholar named Kraisri Nimmanahaeminda, who donated his family home as an example of northern architecture to the Siam Society in Bangkok, has made a detailed study of the *ham yon*, rapidly becoming rare as Western-style houses replace traditional ones. Among other things, he discovered that the size of the lintels was determined by the length of the owner's foot, with a small one being three times the length and a large one four times as long. The designs, of uncertain symbolic intent, are at once decorative and highly varied — often stylized flowers, geometric designs, or cloud-like patterns. Before the carver set about his task, Mr. Kraisri found, a ceremony was held in which the house owner offered food, flowers, and candles to the magic power, inviting it to enter the lintel and assume the role of protector of the house. In his study he commented further:

As the house ages, the ham yon *... become more powerful. Often when an old house is sold, the new owner, before he moves in or dismantles it, will beat the* ham yon *mercilessly in order to destroy the magic accumulated in them under the old owner for it might bode ill for him. This beating of the lintel or 'testicles' is actually a symbolic 'castration.'*

Mural painting detail in Wat Buat Krok Luang in Chiang Mai, late 19th century.

Mr. Kraisri also offers two theories collected from the Thai Yuan, as northern Thais are sometimes known, to explain the peculiar shape of their houses. According to one, "the house is designed to resemble a huge buffalo planted firmly on its pillar-like legs, the body sloping out to massive shoulders supporting the head from which the horns rise. The *ham yon*, above the entrance to the private inner chamber, symbolize the genitals of the beast — the source of its power." The other is more fanciful and also more ominous: it holds that the outward-slanting walls and peaked roof of the house approximates the shape of a Burmese coffin, and that the Thai Yuan were compelled to live in such inauspicious structures when the Burmese conquered them in the mid-16th century as a way of destroying them spiritually.

About 80 per cent of the components in both northern and central houses are prefabricated. There have been various speculations on the reasons for this eminently practical development. One claims that it arose in the workshops of master builders, which also served as schools; since the skills of carpentry were verbal, passed down from generation to generation through apprenticeship, it was more convenient to teach those skills applying to each part of a house in a single place where the various tools were readily available. Moreover, it was economical. When several house orders came in, the sections could be produced by a sort of assembly-line process,

with the gable specialists working in one area, those who made walls in another, and so on.

It is also believed that the vogue for paneling walls — a distinctive feature of classic Thai style — was born in the workshops. According to one theory, these first appeared on houses built for the carpenters themselves as a thrifty way to use left-over wood. Sometimes relatively small pieces were fitted together with narrower bands to hold them in place, sometimes larger ones, both creating pleasing patterns on the otherwise plain walls. When prospective customers saw this innovation at the workshop, they were inspired to have it applied to the houses they ordered. Precisely when the practice became widespread is uncertain, but it may have been relatively recent, as no mention of it is found in accounts by foreign travellers to Ayutthaya toward the end of the 17th century.

Another reason for prefabrication was undoubtedly that it made moving house far simpler. People who settled on the banks of a river or canal, as the majority of Thais did in the past, were regularly plagued by erosion or floods which necessitated a move to a new location; often, too, whole communities were shifted — or decided to shift themselves — for one reason or another, such as war or the availability of better farming land. Thanks to the method of construction, the greater part of a house could be taken down from its framework, stacked

*An 17th-century engraving entitled "A House of a Siamese"
from Simon De La Loubère's account of his visit to
Ayutthaya.*

neatly on barges or buffalo carts, and transported to its new location.

Finally, prefabrication greatly speeded up building, as Western architects have discovered in the present century. This was a matter of particular importance in crowded urban areas like 17th-century Ayutthaya, which had a population of more than a million, and also in early Bangkok; fire was a regular menace in such cities of wood and bamboo houses, and large neighborhoods were often destroyed in a single conflagration. In 1687, Simon de la Loubère was in Ayutthaya on a mission when some 300 houses went up in flame. They were rebuilt within two days on the same location.

In the far south, a very different kind of traditional house developed, also influenced by climatic conditions. It consisted of a single unit, a long hall-like affair, rather than a cluster of rooms, and there was usually no verandah. Windows had flap-like shutters held open with poles outside and closed during monsoon storms. The pillars supporting the house, rarely as high as those elsewhere in Thailand because of high winds, were often set inside large stones in which holes were drilled, thus giving the structure more strength in the sandy, often wet soil. Some prefabrication was practiced with houses made of bamboo, for which the walls were made separately, but not to the extent that it was elsewhere in the country. Smaller houses, nevertheless, could be easily moved by the simple expedient of placing poles under them and lifting the whole structure, posts and all, off its stone supports.

The Thai house usually regarded as the ultimate in classic style is the kind found throughout the central plains, where the Thais achieved their greatest power and sense of cultural identity. Raised on round posts or floating in a river or canal, it has steep roofs with wide decorative bargeboards that rise to a sharp peak in the middle and curve gracefully upward at either end in a decorative feature known in Thai as *ngao*, which was developed from Khmer art during the Sukhothai period and which appears in many forms on religious buildings and palaces, all more elaborate than the version on the domestic house. Leaning slightly inward, possibly to increase the slope of the roof, the panelled walls seem to be straining toward the sky, suggesting in a suitably modest way the more substantial glory of Thai temples. Door thresholds are raised, making the prefabricated walls stronger, and some of the better houses have carved panels below the windows on the outside. Ideally adapted to the climate and to the cultural requirements of its residents, it is also a model of elegant lightness and, as increasing numbers of people are rediscovering, a beautiful creation that meets many modern needs as well as those of the past.

The exact evolution of the central Thai house remains something of a mystery, thanks to the lack of

*Engraving of a Thai house from the French edition of Henri
Mouhot's account of his travels in Thailand, 1858-61.
Following pages: A view of Bangkok, taken in 1900.*

reliable research materials. In Sukhothai, the first Thai capital, both palaces and ordinary homes were constructed of perishable materials — probably bamboo, in the case of the latter — and no trace of either has survived. The same is true for most of Ayutthaya's 400-year history, when even though the kings adopted the Khmer concept of divine rule they continued for centuries to build their own palaces out of wood, reserving stone and masonry for religious structures. Not until toward the end of the 17th century, in the reign of King Narai, were the first enduring royal buildings put up, probably through the influence of Europeans who came at that time.

It is likely, however, that certain features of the central house appeared quite early, in even the simplest bamboo-and-thatch version. High elevation from the ground was a practical necessity in a flat region subject to annual innundation, just as an open platform and a general sense of airiness was a logical answer to a hot, humid climate and the desire to spend as much time as possible outside the sleeping quarters. The steep roof with its long overhangs helped protect the inner room from the heavy rains that came regularly for three or four months out of the year. Moves were frequent among the peasant population in those days, so prefabrication offered both convenience and economy. Finally, according to Thai custom, a son went to live with his wife's family after marriage — a practice that not only provided an extra worker for the family fields but also eliminated the conflicts between daughter and mother-in-law — and this led naturally to the so-called "cluster house" in which several rooms share the same platform.

We do not know, however, just when the wooden central house acquired the distinctive appearance by which it is recognized today. De la Loubère, whose *Historical Relation of the Kingdom of Siam* is generally regarded as the best source of information on life in Ayutthaya at the peak of its prosperity, had this to say on the houses of the late 17th century:

If the Siamese are plain in their habits, they are not less so in their homes, in their furniture, and in their food: rich in a general poverty because they know how to content themselves with a little. Their houses are small, but surrounded with pretty large grounds. Hurdles of cleft bamboo, oftentimes not close compacted, do make the floors, walls, and roofs thereof. The piles, on which they are erected to avoid the innundation, are bamboos as thick as one's leg, and about 13 foot above the ground, by reason that the waters do sometimes rise as much as that. There is never more than four or six, on which they do lay other bamboos instead of beams. The stairs are a ladder of bamboo, which hangs on the outside like the ladder of a windmill.

De la Loubère also noted that high court officials

*A floating house, photographed by Robert Lenz in Bangkok
at the turn of the century.*

lived in wooden houses, which they were careful to make "less exalted than the palaces [of the King]," and scotches the report that "no person may be higher in his own house than the King of Siam when he passes through the street mounted on his elephant" — an impossibility, he points out, considering the fact that the houses were erected on such high piles.

Nowhere in this detailed commentary, it will be noted, is there any mention of ornamentation, in particular of the wide curving bargeboards and paneled walls that are now such prominent features of the classic house. On the other hand, in apparent contradiction, de la Loubère's work does include an engraving labelled "A House of a Siamese" which though it has walls apparently made of woven bamboo is also adorned by roof decorations strikingly similar to those seen on temples, not only on the eaves but also at either end of the roof. Whether this rendering is realistic or whether the artist embellished his sketches (as those who depicted the Thais themselves certainly did) must remain unknown; in support of the latter, however, is the fact that no such domestic Thai house appears in any mural painting of a slightly later period.

Only 75 years after De la Loubère's book appeared, Ayutthaya fell to the Burmese. Virtually the entire city was destroyed by fire, especially the bamboo and wooden structures that had housed the great majority of its population, leaving almost as much mystery surrounding their precise architecture as that which shrouds the ordinary homes of Sukhothai. Some authorities believe that the house we know today developed only at the very end of Ayutthaya, and possibly not until the Bangkok period, which began in 1782. If so, then the development must have been remarkably fast for the structures can be seen in numerous murals painted in the early 19th century with all their classic features on display, looking very much like a well-established part of the landscape.

Various kinds of houses appear in these paintings, as they still do in many parts of rural Thailand. The smallest is a single unit with bedroom, kitchen, verandah, and open platform, all of course elevated on posts. More common are the cluster houses, where as many as five bedrooms are arranged around the central platform, with the owner's room always occupying the most important place. Along the banks of rivers and canals, the structure may serve as both house and shop, with the bedroom and kitchen in the rear and the open front used to display merchandise; a single piece of some light material such as thatch covers the front at night and is opened during business hours. Finally, there are the floating houses that attracted so much comment from early European visitors. These, too, are twin houses in which the family lives in the rear and trades in the one facing the water. Architecturally, they are the same as the

View of Bangkok around 1900 from the Golden Mount, then the highest point in the city.

others, except that the planks of the floor are not as tightly fitted to allow for more movement as the stream rises and falls.

Simple as it may appear to an outsider, the Thai house embodies a complex accretion of symbols and beliefs, covering almost every aspect of its construction and arrangement of living space. Before building commences, the future resident must consult an astrologer to determine the most suitable month. This will usually be January, March, April, August, November, or December, though it may vary in particular cases. Once the month has been settled, further calculations are required to determine the proper day and time to begin placing the pillars in the ground. Traditionally, the best days for the initial post raising are Thursday, Friday and Saturday.

Alignment of the house on the plot of ground is equally important. S.J. Tambiah, an anthropologist who worked in Thailand, made this observation on the points of the compass in a northeast village, but they apply also in the north and central region:

East is auspicious, represents life, is sacred ... and is the direction of the rising sun. East is also, when one faces north, the direction of the right hand and represents male sex. West is inauspicious, represents death, impurity, and the setting sun. It also represents the left hand and the female sex. North is auspicious and is associated with the elephant, an auspicious animal because of its size, natural strength and its associations with royalty and Buddhist mythology. South is of neutral value.

Based on these values, according to his study, "Ideally a person entering the house would face the north and the entrance platform is at the southern end and the sleeping room at the northern end. The directions can be reversed. Never must the sleeping room be placed in the west. The kitchen and the washing place are also always on the western side of the house." In some cases, nature interferes with these arrangements, particularly when the house is on a waterway, as was frequently the case in the past. Here, however, tradition is accommodating: water is believed to be auspicious enough to counteract any taboo, even a westerly orientation.

The size of the house determines the number of posts, but however many are used there must be an odd number of spaces between them, generally either three or five (just as there must also be an odd number of steps on the ladder or stair leading to the platform). Thus:
○ (1) ○ (2) ○ (3) ○ (4) ○ (5) ○
But never:
○ (1) ○ (2) ○ (3) ○ (4) ○
The posts are carefully selected for strength and smoothness, and often auspicious names like king, diamond, and happiness are inscribed on them. In

*"Interior of a Siamese House," from F.A. Neale's account of
his stay in Thailand in 1850.*

central Thailand, the two most important are called *saaw eg* ("first or primary post") and *saaw khwan* ("post containing the spiritual essense"); usually the *saaw eg* will be part of the support for the east side of the main bedroom, across from the *saaw khwan*. On the day these two are placed in the ground — chosen by the builder on the basis of their perfection — a ceremony is performed to ask the spirit guarding the land for permission, with offerings of such delicacies as betelnut, young coconuts, boiled eggs, bananas, and Thai desserts, all placed beside the hole. Later, a special little house, also raised on a pole, will be put somewhere on the property to serve as a spiritual abode, supplied with regular provisions and burning incense sticks. Usually this will be a miniature of the classic Thai house, though wealthier families may choose an ornate, multi-colored affair that resembles a temple building.

Both the first and second posts to be raised are decorated beforehand with young banana shrubs, stalks of sugar cane, and lengths of sacred colored cloth, and gold leaf is applied to the top of each. In some places a piece of clothing belonging to the male of the household is tied to the first post and one belonging to his wife to the second. When these items are removed during construction, the plants often become a part of the garden. The men who carry the posts to the site and place them in the holes are chosen for having auspicious-sounding names, or

at least given them for the duration of the ceremony; among the popular ones are *Phet* (diamond), *Thong Kham* (pure gold), and *Ngoen* (silver).

The arrangement of the various areas in the house is also a matter of tradition. The highest is the main bedroom, generally about 40 centimeters above the verandah, which in turn is some 40 centimeters above the open platform. Doors and windows must always open inwards. The shelf or altar holding the family Buddha images faces east, and the kitchen, being a place of no spiritual significance, is on the west; the washing area is on the lowest level. Toilets, when they exist, are usually in a separate structure elsewhere in the compound, though chamber pots are still widely used in many rural areas.

The date for moving in calls for further astrological calculations and may or may not coincide with the owner's wishes or even actual completion of the house. Monks are always invited in the morning to receive food, thus bringing merit to the owner and assuring his happiness, and a senior priest will ritually bless each of the main rooms.

The exterior simplicity of the traditional Thai house — besides the curving bargeboards, the only decoration usually found is the piece of carved wood under the windows and perhaps some more carving on the main door frame — is reflected in its furnishings. Since family activities customarily take place on the floor, there is always an ample supply of

The Chao Phya River at Bangkok, photographed by Robert Lenz in 1900 when floating houses were common.

woven reed mats for sleeping or sitting. More prosperous families may have low beds and tables with curved legs in Chinese style, and there may also be a low dressing table, used at floor level; the bedroom also generally contains a chest or cupboard to store clothes and other possessions. Water for the bathroom and kitchen is kept in large jars, sometimes glazed and decorated with dragons or other motifs. The kitchen contains a charcoal stove and a screened cabinets for dishes and foodstuffs.

Some color and greenery is provided by pot plants on the open platform, selected for fragrance, beauty, and names that in Thai suggest good fortune. Jasmine is a perennial favorite in the first category, and crotons and caladiums are prominent among the last; there is a large category of plants known by Thais as *wahn*, or lucky, each with its own auspicious-sounding name, and several pots of these can be found on nearly every platform.

The garden surrounding the house is mainly utilitarian, though traditional belief may also play a role. If there is a star gooseberry (*ma-yom* in Thai) it will be planted in front of the house since *yom* means "admiration" and will thus attract people to the owners; similarly, a jackfruit (*kha-nun*) will be grown behind since *nun* suggests the idea of support. Somewhere there will be an area for the herbs and spices essential to any Thai kitchen: basil and mint, chilli peppers and lemon grass, ginger and coriander.

Coconut palms are common, as are such fruits trees as mango, tamarind, guava, and rose apple. An old-fashioned garden will also contain a number of plants whose roots, leaves, or flowers can be used for medicinal purposes.

Not surprisingly, there are certain plants which tradition says must not be grown. Frangipani (*plumeria*) is taboo because its Thai name, *lan-tom*, sounds like *ra-tom*, which means "sorrow." The Bodhi tree is forbidden because of its association with Buddhism and most other members of the Ficus family because they are believed to harbor spirits. *Bombax malabaricum*, a native tree whose orange-red flowers are used in soup by northerners, is frowned upon for two compelling reasons: its soft wood is popular with coffin-makers and also in depictions of Buddhist hell unfaithful husbands and wives are shown climbing its trunk with a tiger in hot pursuit.

At the time P.A. Thompson came to Thailand, houses of the kind described here were as characteristic of the landscape as the fabulous Buddhist temples. Within a generation they had almost vanished from Bangkok and were becoming increasingly rare in the countryside as new building materials and new lifestyles found favor. Only in relatively recent years has there been a renewed appreciation of their beauty and practicality, and it has come, paradoxically, from the same affluent group which was the first to abandon the old style.

HOUSES FLOATING AND ON TERRA FIRMA

In the past, most communities were located on rivers or canals and many of the houses were literally in the water, either floating or anchored on posts. As these pictures show, the old custom is still followed in many parts of the country.

Wood was the traditional building material in old Thailand, employed on both Thai-style houses and those that later displayed Western influences (following pages). Roofs were generally tiled or thatched, steeply sloped, and had broad eaves to protect the interior from sunlight and rain. Elaborate fretwork adorned many buildings of the late 19th century and early 20th centuries.

THIS PAGE: *Floating houses in Uthai Thani Province.*
FACING PAGE: *(Top left) Traditional floating houses. (Top right) A reconstructed building over water at the Ancient City. (Center and bottom) Structures along the Chao Phya River at Uthai Thani.*
FOLLOWING PAGES LEFT: *Traditional Thai houses in Angthong and Ayutthaya Provinces.*
FOLLOWING PAGES RIGHT: *Examples of houses, traditonal and otherwise, from various parts of the country.*
PAGES 66-67: *A range of Thai rooftops, thatched and tiled.*

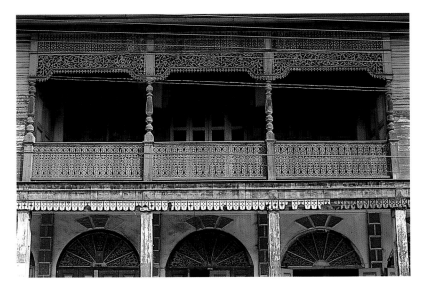

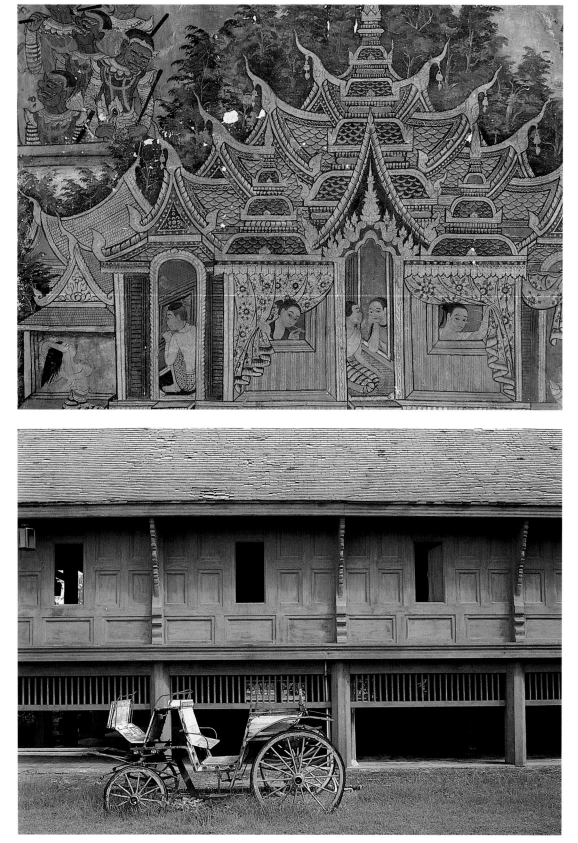

PALACE OF A PRINCE

The Prince of Lampang's palace, known as the Ho Kham or "gilded hall," was built in the provincial capital of Lampang during the early Bangkok period. The original building was pulled down in the 1930's; the one shown here was reconstructed from old photographs at an outdoor museum called the Ancient City just outside Bangkok, where numerous classic buildings and careful reproductions from Thailand's past are displayed in a large area. The residence, in northern style, is made entirely of timber without nails and raised off the ground on large posts.

LEFT ABOVE: *Detail from a mural painting in the Vihan Laikham at Wat Phra Singh in Chiang Mai. The roof decorations are similar to those on the Prince of Lampang's palace.*
LEFT BELOW: *Side of the Prince of Lampang's residence, with a horse cart of a type still used in Lampang.*
RIGHT: *The residence of the Prince of Lampang. The finials at the top of the roofs, known as* chofas, *were more commonly used on temples but sometimes appeared on royal palaces.*

NON-WOODEN PALACES

In Sukhothai and during the early part of the Ayutthaya period, palaces as well as the homes of ordinary citizens were made of wood and other perishable materials, stone and masonry being reserved for religious buildings. This began to change in Ayutthaya, particularly in the 17th century, when more and more royal buildings of solid construction appeared. By the time Bangkok became the capital it was an established practice, with many Western architectural techniques being employed.

ABOVE AND LEFT: *Brick and cement began to be employed in palace construction in the Ayutthaya period and this practice continued in Bangkok. The Chantatakasem Palace in Ayutthaya shown here was the customary residence of the Crown Princes. Destroyed by the Burmese when they captured the city in 1767, it was partially rebuilt by King Rama IV in the mid-19th century.*

RIGHT, ABOVE AND BELOW: *Views of Khao Wang Palace in Petchaburi, built on a hilltop in the 19th century by King Rama IV, who indulged a fondness for astronomy from an observation tower in the compound. The palace has recently been extensively restored by the Fine Arts Department.*

MONKS' QUARTERS

A Thai *wat,* or religious complex, is divided into two parts: one containing the public buildings where prayers are chanted and various ceremonies held and the other containing living quarters for the resident monks. While the buildings in the latter may on occasion be ornate, they are more often plain wooden traditional structures, similar in most ways to domestic houses of the outside world.

LEFT, ABOVE AND BELOW: *Monks' quarters with ornate stucco decorations at a temple in Nakorn Phanom, near the border of Thailand and Laos.*

ABOVE: *Rooftops of the quarters where the monks live at Wat Mahathat in Bangkok.*
LEFT: *A temple building and a* sala *on a canal in Ayutthaya.*

A KING'S RESIDENCE

This house dates from the latter part of the 18th century and served as the residence of King Rama I before he came to the throne and founded the Chakri Dynasty. He donated the structure to Wat Rakhang Kositaram in Dhonburi to serve as a repository for sacred scriptures and, after becoming king, ordered extensive renovations, among them the carved doors and the mural paintings on the interior walls.

The house consists of three units joined together, with a number of its architectural features altered when it was reconstructed in the temple compound. The murals were the work of Phra Acharn Nak, one of the few early artists whose names are known today, and depict kneeling Thai divinities as well as scenes from the *Ramakien* epic.

FAR LEFT: *Interior of King Rama I's former residence containing a large scripture cabinet with gold-and-black lacquer decorations; the mural paintings on the walls and the traditional motifs on the columns were done after the house had been presented to the temple.*
LEFT ABOVE: *Carved and gilded doors on the house with ornamental eave brackets.*
LEFT BELOW: *View of the prang of Wat Rakhang through a window of the building.*

BAAN SAO NAK

Baan Sao Nak, which means "the house of numerous pillars," stands in the northern city of Lampang and is the home of Khunying Walai Leelanuch, principal of the Lampang Kallayanee School. Built in a mixture of Lanna Thai and Burmese styles, it is believed to have been originally erected by the present owner's grandparents, who were of Burmese origin, in 1896. It stands on 116 teak pillars, giving rise to its popular name.

Starting in 1964 and continuing until 1974, extensive repairs were carried out on the house. Concrete plinths were added to the pillars to prevent further sinking of the large structure, the wooden floorboards of the porch were replaced with tiles, and the gutter, originally made from teak carved as a channel, was covered with galvanized iron.

In 1987, Khunying Walai decided to replace an old rice barn which had been a part of the compound with another built in traditional style and resting on 24 pillars. The barn was consecrated in an elaborate ceremony involving ancient northern rituals in March of 1988.

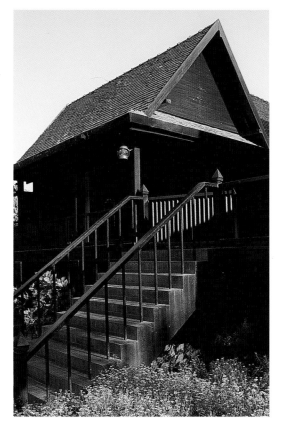

LEFT ABOVE: *The front of Baan Sao Nak, showing the entrance stairway.*

FAR LEFT BELOW: *Part of the verandah and the living room, with typical Thai furnishings.*

ABOVE: *The rice barn, a traditional feature of northern compounds.*

LEFT: *An earthernware jar, still made in the north, which is kept filled with cool water for thirsty passers-by.*

FAR LEFT: *The entrance stairway to the house.*

ABOVE: *The kitchen of the Kamthieng House, with a collection of typical cooking pots, glutinous rice baskets, and other kitchen utensils.*
RIGHT: *The verandah, on which are displayed an elephant howdah, a rice container, and a bamboo device for carrying water jars.*

THE KAMTHIENG HOUSE

The Kamthieng House stands in the Bangkok compound of the Siam Society, a scholarly organization established in 1904, and serves today as an ethnological museum. Dating from the middle of the 19th century, the traditional northern-style house formerly stood on the east bank of the Ping River in Chiang Mai. It was donated to the Society in the 1960's by Khun Kraisri Nimmanahaeminda, a business-man and scholar from Chiang Mai, and named in honor of his grandmother, Nang Kamthieng Anusarasundara, who was born in the house. The structure contains a living area, a covered verandah, an open platform, and a kitchen. Connected by a walkway is a teak rice granary which the Society also acquired in Chiang Mai. Various items used in daily life are displayed in the buildings.

ABOVE: *Gables of the house, with typical northern* galae *decorations.*
RIGHT: *The rice granary, under which is a buffalo cart commonly used by farmers in the region.*

TRADITIONS RENEWED

S. Reuycharoeng in Angthong employs a large number of skilled craftsmen to produce traditional Thai houses. The business has been responsible for numerous homes in various parts of Thailand, particularly Bangkok, and several years ago sent a team of builders to Monte Carlo, where they assembled a pavilion for a wealthy resident who had admired the structures on a visit.

LEFT: *On a field in Angthong, workers make the components of a Thai house, nearly all of which are prefabricated and then assembled on the building site.*
RIGHT: *Home of S. Reuycharoeng in Angthong. The house serves as a model for customers wishing to select details of construction and decoration.*

TRADITIONS ADAPTED

In a village near the old capital of Ayutthaya, dozens of doors, paneled walls, gables, and other components of the classic Thai house are neatly stacked under a simple shelter overlooking a rice field. Fifty years ago, perhaps less, all would have been destined for one of the farming families in the area, taking their place in a traditional village setting. Today most will end up in Bangkok gardens, overlooked by towering office blocks and condominiums. Some may even go much further — to Hawaii, perhaps, or to the south of France, there to shelter strangers who have never heard of the village where they were created but whose imagination has been fired by a glimpse of Thailand's traditional domestic architecture being used as a backdrop for modern living.

Some date this development from the spring of 1959 when Jim Thompson, the American who revived the Thai silk industry, moved into a Thai-style house on a Bangkok *klong*. It was not the only such structure to be seen in the capital at the time, nor the largest: several members of the royal family could point to impressive ancestral homes in their spacious compounds, and the distinctive peaked roofs were then still fairly common in older neighborhoods, though their owners often regarded them as old-fashioned and uncomfortable. What made the Thompson house different from most of these was the fact that he had adapted the classic concepts to the needs of a contemporary lifestyle and shown in a dramatic way

The Jim Thompson house in the evening, showing the living room overlooking a terrace. Glazed and pierced 18th-century Chinese tiles are set into the balustrade.

83

Rooftops of the Jim Thompson House.
Opposite: Carved wooden doors from Ayutthaya,
probably 18th century, with a design of plants and birds.

that they remained practical as well as beautiful.

"Jim Thompson's Thai House" appears on most tourist itineraries today, and hundreds of visitors come weekly to admire his extensive collection of Asian art displayed in it. The majority are equally impressed by the house itself, rising with serene elegance out of a lush garden, though few perhaps understand the numerous ways — some subtle, some drastic — in which Thompson modified the traditional architecture to achieve his goal. Residents, Thai as well as foreign, inspected his innovations more carefully, and many were inspired to emulate them, not only in Bangkok but also in other parts of the country. It may be overstating the case to say that Jim Thompson performed the same service for Thai domestic houses that he did for the country's silk, but there can be little doubt that he was responsible in large part for the subsequent boom in such structures, prompting buyers to seek out surviving houses and bringing a flood of orders to carpenters skilled in the old crafts like those in Ayutthaya.

As more than a few have discovered, the transformation involves more than merely assembling the components thus acquired. The classic house was well suited to the simple needs of rural life in the past. It was open and airy, had space below for the family's domestic animals, and, with its arrangement of separate rooms around a platform, could accommodate various members in a way that re-

flected their status. Most of these advantages became either irrelevant or downright inconvenient in an urban setting. Privacy (an alien concept to Thai villagers) assumed a far greater importance when strangers as well as friendly neighbors might be peering in; conveniences like airconditioning, bathrooms, and modern kitchens, essential to sophisticated city dwellers, had to somehow be installed; moreover, many wanted easier passage from room to room than the traditional arrangement allowed.

The problem, essentially, was how to adapt a traditional house to these requirements without destroying its architectural distinction. Some unhappy hybrids have resulted, blending various styles incongruously or failing to respect the proportions that contribute so importantly to the elegance of the true Thai house. But as the following pages show, a number have been notably successful, even when apparently violating basic tenets. Jim Thompson, for example, insisted on an enclosed stairwell, linked the assorted houses by connecting passageways, and reversed the walls of the drawing room so that the carvings under the windows faced inward. Others have incorporated swimming pools, Jacuzzis, steam baths, and an assortment of other decidedly non-traditional amenities. Yet in doing so, they have nonetheless managed to preserve the basic Thai flavor, so that the houses retain their artistic integrity while also offering the comforts their owners desire.

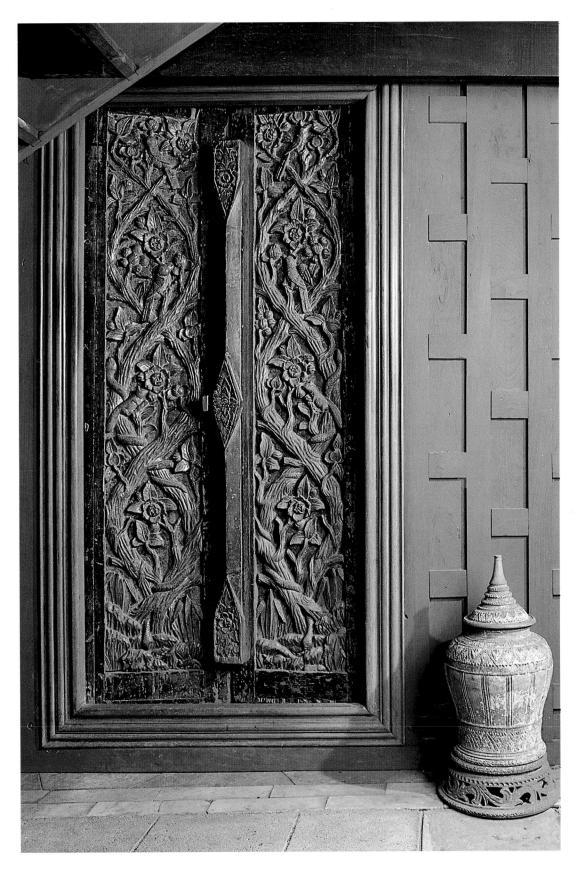

THE HOUSE ON THE KLONG

Four old central Thai houses and part of a fifth were used in the construction of Jim Thompson's famous house, located on a canal the center of modern Bangkok. The largest and oldest, dating from around 1800, forms the drawing room and came from a silk weaving village across the canal, as did the one housing the kitchen; others were brought downriver from a village near the old capital of Ayutthaya. In assembling them, Thompson enclosed the staircase in a marble-floored hallway, joined the rooms with connecting roofs, added modern baths, and reversed the walls of the drawing room so that the carvings below the windows' faced inward.

Work was started on the house in September of 1958 and it was completed in April of the following year. Since Thompson's disappearance in 1967, it has been maintained as a museum, with the proceeds going for various projects concerned with Thai culture.

LEFT: *The dining room. The porcelain is Annamese and was made in the Ming Dynasty, while the chandelier is from a 19th-century Bangkok palace.*

RIGHT: *Six interior views: (Top left) Seated sandstone Buddha in Lopburi-Khmer style, 13th century, flanked by 12th-century Khmer figures of Siva and Uma in limestone. (Top right) Annamese and Chinese porcelains in the dining room. (Middle left) In the entrance hall. (Middle right) The master bedroom, overlooking the central terrace. (Bottom left) Stair hall, hung with Thai temple paintings on cloth. (Bottom right) Doors from an old Chinese pawnshop, dividing the living room from the bedroom wing.*

FAR LEFT: *The living room of the Thompson house, now open to the public as a museum. Wooden Burmese nats hang in the alcoves, which were originally windows.*

ABOVE: *The study. Among the pictures on the wall are 17th-century French engravings of Thais in Ayutthaya, while the limestone Buddha in the alcove is of the Dvaravati period (6th-10th century).*

LEFT: *Close-up of the Dvaravati image.*

ABOVE: *Carved doors of the Thompson house. The black and white marble tiles came from an old Bangkok palace.*
LEFT: *Entrance to the stair-hall, with the kitchen on the right. Architecturally, this would be the back of the house.*
RIGHT: *The terrace, paved with 18th-century bricks from Ayutthaya. On the right can be seen the roof of the* sala *facing Klong Maha Nag.*

ELEGANT ENTERTAINING

Mrs. Connie Mangskau, one of Bangkok's leading dealers in decorative arts, was inspired to build a Thai-style house for entertaining by her friend Jim Thompson, who also helped with the design. A number of old houses, mostly acquired near Ayutthaya, were used on three sides of a raised platform overlooking the garden. Mrs. Mangskau's daughter, Mrs. Joanna Cross, who continues to operate the business founded by her mother, lives in one part of the house, which is furnished with an exceptionally fine collection of Thai, Chinese, and Khmer art.

LEFT: *The living room, which occupies one side of the upper terrace. Among the items on display are a large Thai bed, a pair of Burmese priests in lacquered wood, an ivory betel nut set and a tapestry-size Thai painting on cloth.*

ABOVE: *Front of the house showing the large terrace which Mrs. Mangskau and Mrs. Cross use for entertaining.*

LEFT: *Chinese figurines displayed on a carved bed under the house; on the wall in the back is a woodcarving from the gable of a northern temple.*

ABOVE: *A view of the interior of Tula Bunnag's house. Among the furnishings are a carved wooden cabinet, a gold-and-black lacquer chest for storing manuscript books, and a fine dressing table.*

VINTAGE STRUCTURES

The structures that comprise Tula Bunnag's house were mostly old ones acquired near Ayutthaya, brought to Bangkok and assembled in 1965. Four are arranged around the central platform, and a fifth was added later at a lower level for a son's family; the entrance stair has been left uncovered in the traditional style.

A gifted woodcarver, Tula Bannag provided many decorative features for the houses himself, among them window carvings that depict the animals of the years in which he and his wife were born. His fine mother-of-pearl inlay work can also be seen on many objects displayed in the houses.

ABOVE: *Buddha images belonging to the family.*
RIGHT: *The Buddha Room, off the central platform of the house, where homage is paid each day to the various images.*

ABOVE: *House built for one of the Bunnag sons, adjacent to the main dwelling; Tula Bunnag did the woodcarvings under the windows.*
LEFT: *The Bunnag house from the garden.*

TRADITIONAL —
WITH A MODERN FLAIR

The Bangkok home of Patsri and Jean-Michael Beurdeley gives the impression of being an old northern-style house which has been moved to the capital. Actually it was entirely new when it was built some 14 years ago, though most of the woodcarvings used in its decorations are antiques collected in the north of Thailand.

A small swimming pool has been incorporated into the design, around which are four separate units containing a living room, a dining room, a master bedroom, and guest rooms; the kitchen is located downstairs. Francois Catroux, a Paris-based decorator, designed the living room, using a parquet floor with one sunken area for a display of plants; the panelled walls of the dining room were the creation of a Bangkok antique dealer, Somkid Thanapoomikul.

ABOVE: *Painted cabinet, on which is displayed a fragment of a Khmer stone head.*

LEFT: *Painted doors and panels from northern Thailand, used in the guest bedroom. The paintings depict guardian figures surrounded by Thai motifs.*

LEFT: *The Beurdeley house from the entrance courtyard, showing the distinctive* northern galae *decorations on the roof ends.*

LEFT BELOW: *The swimming pool, which has been set into the platform around which the various houses are arranged.*

RIGHT: *A view of the platform, showing a long drum used in many northern ceremonies.*

LEFT ABOVE: *A low couch made from pieces of old carved wood over which are panels from a northern temple. A painted cabinet to hold manuscript books stands against the left wall.*
BELOW FAR LEFT: *An elephant howdah.*
LEFT: *A carved lintel showing monkey gods.*
ABOVE: *The dining room with a Chinese scroll and covered brass bowls in the shape of sprouting coconuts. The wall panels are new, supplied by a Bangkok art dealer.*

FOLLOWING PAGES: *The living room features a sunken area for potted plants, low cushions covered in Thai cotton, a Thai table, and two northern manuscript cabinets.*

ON THE CHAO PHYA

The Thai-style house of Achille Clarac, former French ambassador to Thailand, and his son, Henri, is located on the Chao Phya River. A thick riverside stand of nipa palms screens the front of the property, which preserves a rural atmosphere though it can be reached by boat from the center of Bangkok in a relatively short time. The main house consists of a living room, dining room, and two bedrooms built around an open platform; a guest pavilion overlooks a pool in the extensive garden, planted with a large variety of tropical shrubs and trees. Due to high river tides, the owners have devised a complex hydraulics system to protect the garden from flooding by sometimes saline water.

LEFT ABOVE: *A wooden walkway leads from the river landing through a thick growth of nipa palms to the compound.*
LEFT: *An entrance pavilion stands at the top of the steps to the central platform.*

ABOVE: *Paved with laterite blocks, the area under the house opens directly on to the garden and provides a cool sitting area. Old Thai water jars are planted with water lilies and lotus.*

LEFT: *One of the numerous pumps used in keeping the compound free of river floods is concealed under a small Thai-style structure, thus adding to the visual appeal of the garden. The lawn is planted with hardy, broad-leaved Malaysian grass which thrives in heavy, sometimes water-logged soil.*

FOLLOWING PAGES: *The garden of the Clarac compound, densely planted with palms, heliconias, and other tropical specimens; the guest pavilion, adorned by an old pediment, can be seen on the right.*

TRADITIONS REVAMPED

The four Thai-style houses and garden pavilion that comprise this grouping, built in the same Bangkok compound with a Western-style family home, were constructed by the S. Reuycharoeng company of Angthong described on page 78. Carpenters skilled in the old crafts lived on the site during assembly of the prefabricated sections.

On one part of the main house containing the dining room, a base of laterite stone and modern glass windows was employed to allow more light into the interior and also to facilitate airconditioning. Among the other modern features is a marble bathroom complete with a Jacuzzi and steamroom, in which natural lighting comes through translucent glass bricks.

In addition to the two main houses, joined by a wooden deck, a separate structure consisting of two other houses contains the guest rooms, kitchen, and servants' quarters.

FAR LEFT: *Living room. The furniture here and elsewhere in the house was made by Khun Chantaka Puranananda, a Bangkok designer.*
ABOVE: *The master bedroom; the bedspread and cushions are Thai silk.*
LEFT: *A view of the guest wing, which also contains the kitchen and servants' quarters.*

LEFT ABOVE: *The dining room. A laterite base has been added to allow the installation of windows that protrude and provide a view of the garden.*
LEFT BELOW: *A view of the bathroom.*
BELOW: *The spirit house.*

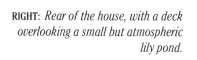

RIGHT: *Rear of the house, with a deck overlooking a small but atmospheric lily pond.*

THAI-WESTERN COMPROMISE

The owner of the house shown on these pages wanted to live in a Western style dwelling yet also enjoy the open elegance of Thailand's classic domestic architecture. The problem was solved by Alicia de Guzman, a Filipina architect who has worked in Bangkok for many years, through using Thai-style structures for entertainment areas, guest quarters, and the kitchen and connecting them with a modern house at the back by way of an open-sided lobby. A system of ponds and waterways surrounds the buildings, and privacy has been achieved through planting trees and stands of bamboo.

LEFT: *Entrance steps, leading to a traditional pavilion where guests are received.*
ABOVE: *Open platform, with exceptionally broad teak planks forming the floor.*
RIGHT: *A view of the house and grounds.*

LEFT ABOVE: *A large painting framed in old wood, overlooking a dining area; prehistoric pots stand on the shelf above the bench, and the cushions are covered with cotton made by northern hill tribes.*

LEFT BELOW: *The area connecting various elements of the house is open and sparsely furnished, cooled by an old ceiling fan. The reclining chairs are typical of the furniture that appeared in Thai home with the rise of Western influences in the late 19th century.*

ABOVE: *The music room, showing an old harp, a handsome manuscript cabinet with gold and black lacquer paintings, and a finely carved xylophone used in traditional Thai orchestras.*

RIGHT: *Entrance to the main room in the Thai-style part of the house; above the door is a large painting on wood. The matchstick blinds can be lowered during storms to protect the interior from winds and rains.*

117

A COLLECTOR'S HAVEN

Soon after he moved to Thailand from America, James Bastabel began collecting coconut scrapers, ingenious devices carved in the shape of various animals on which the workers sat while removing the husk with the aid of a metal projection. Rarely made today, the scrapers were often beautifully carved and represented the twelve animals of the Chinese calendar. Bastabel specialized in rabbit-shaped scrapers and eventually formed an impressive collection of several dozen — some in plain wood, others covered with lacquer — which he incorporated effectively in the decoration of his Bangkok house.

LEFT: *Dining room of the collector's house, in which coconut scrapers have been placed on glass shelves to create an effective wall; the wooden figure in the foreground is Burmese.*

ABOVE: *The living room; on the Thai table are lacquered wooden animals from the north, and in the background can be seen a pair of wooden* chofa, *finials from Thai temples.*

LEFT: *Two coconut scrapers in the shape of rabbits and a piece of Thai silk from the Neold collection.*

ART STUDIO AND HOME

Having enjoyed a traditional Thai *sala* in their garden for several years, Khun Venica Vil's parents brought the units that comprise this Thai house down from Ayutthaya in 1961 and reassembled them on their Bangkok property. All are around 80 to 100 years old. Three units are arranged around a pond, connected by walkways. The largest serves as a studio for Khun Venica's graphic design company, while she and her husband live in the other rooms.

FAR LEFT: *The studio of Khun Venica's design company.*
ABOVE: *Two units of the house, overlooking a central pond.*
LEFT: *Verandah of the house containing the living quarters.*

ABOVE: *Verandah of the house. Thai-style lighting fixtures hang from the ceiling, while the carved wooden screen on the left is from India.*
RIGHT: *The bathroom.*

ABOVE: *A portion of the verandah outside the art studio; a traditional Thai painting hangs on the rear wall above two old ship's lanterns on a Thai table.*

LEFT: *The living room, containing an old dressing table in red lacquer.*

THE THEO MEIER HOUSE

Theo Meier was a Swiss-born painter who spent much of his life in Bali, where his Gauguinesque work attracted wide interest among art collectors. He moved to Thailand in the 1960's at the invitation of Prince Sanidh Rangsit, an old friend, and settled with his Thai wife Laiad in Chiang Mai, building a remarkable house on the bank of the Ping River. Since Meier's death, his widow has continued to live in the house where they entertained a constant stream of admiring guests.

The main house consists of a large verandah overlooking the river, where most of the social life took place, and three bedrooms; there is also a guest house composed of three rooms and a *sala* just inside the gate. Another pavilion was later added to the compound, adjacent to Meier's riverside studio.

ABOVE: *View of the guest pavilion showing the elegant roof-top decoration that defines it as Chiang Mai.*
RIGHT: *Courtyard of house, paved with laterite blocks and softened with lush tropical planting. One of Theo Meier's paintings can be seen on the wall of the entrance area.*

ABOVE: *The riverside pavilion, showing columns painted with typical northern motifs in gold. Locally woven cotton is used on cushions and as a tablecloth. The triangular marks on the doors were placed there by the presiding priest during the ceremony to bless the pavilion.*

LEFT: *Dining table on verandah of the main house. On the wall hangs one of Theo Meier's paintings of Chiang Mai orchids.*

130

LEFT: *Assorted examples of woodcarvings on the various houses in the compound, most of them are the work of contemporary Chiang Mai artisans.*

RIGHT ABOVE: *Part of the main house in its jungle-like setting of vine-hung trees and tall native bamboo.*

RIGHT BELOW: *Verandah of the main house, looking toward the entrance. The footed red-lacquer tray is northern Thai, while the patterned cloths are Indonesian.*

NORTHERN HOLIDAY HOUSE

Located on the outskirts of a village on the Ping River, about 15 kilometers from Chiang Mai, this northern-style house was built by a Bangkok couple as a holiday retreat. It consists of a main dwelling, separate guest quarters, and a pavilion, all on a raised platform overlooking the river. Both old and new elements were used in the construction.

ABOVE: *View of the Ping River.*
LEFT ABOVE: *Dining pavilion on the river.*
LEFT BELOW: *General view of the house, showing an old northern buffalo cart in the garden.*

ABOVE LEFT: *The bedroom. An old wood-carving has been used to form a dramatic headboard for the traditional Thai bed.*
ABOVE RIGHT: *The living room, in which local handwoven cloth has been used to colorful effect.*
LEFT: *A northern water jar with a dipper, often placed outside homes to provide refreshment for thirsty strangers.*

CHIANG MAI RUSTIC

The rustic Chiang Mai home of Somphan and Nongkran Suanduenchai, owners of the Indigo Restaurant and Gallery and collectors of northern Thai textiles, consists of four nothern-style structures, around 60 to 80 years old: the main house, a guest house, a rice barn, and a kitchen and servants' quarters. Chiang Mai is the traditional center of Thai handicrafts, ranging from woodcarving to lacquer, and the house contains many examples among its furnishings, such as handwoven cloth, baskets, and other items typical of a northern home that has been relatively untouched by Western influences.

LEFT ABOVE: *Main house of the Suanduenchai family, showing the steps leading to the entrance platform; this house and others in the compound were acquired in the Chiang Mai area and moved to the site when the original family home was destroyed by fire some years ago.*
LEFT: *Area below the guest house used for weaving cotton.*

ABOVE: *The road from Chiang Mai to Lamphun, on which the house is located.*
RIGHT: *View of the guest house from the platform of the main dwelling. The jar beside the entrance gate contains water used by guests to wash their feet when arriving; a papaya tree can be seen growing at the bottom of the stairs.*

LEFT: *Dining area in the main house, located on the covered but otherwise open platform at the top of the entrance stairs. The lamp shades are fish traps, found in most parts of Thailand, while the elephant plaque above the door came from a northern buffalo cart; an old Thai cabinet stands against the wall inside the house.*

ABOVE, LEFT AND RIGHT: *Two of the three bedrooms in the house. The textiles are cotton, in traditional patterns, while the carved dressing table is of northern workmanship.*

ON THE BEACH

Hua Hin, on the Gulf of Thailand, became a popular resort in the 1920's when the southern railway line made it easily accessible to Bangkok. The King built a summer palace there, and many members of the Thai aristocracy followed to spend the hot-season months. The holiday compound pictured here consists of five separate Thai houses, some old and some new, erected in the late 1970's by Khun Chantaka Puranananda on land belonging to his family. The furnishings came from Pure Design, Khun Chantaka's interior decoration company in Bangkok.

ABOVE AND RIGHT: *Views of the tiled terrace shaded by casuarina trees.*
FAR RIGHT: *The house as seen from the beach at high tide.*

FOREIGN INFLUENCES

Robert Hunter, an Englishman who arrived in Bangkok in 1824 and became the capital's most influential foreign resident for nearly 20 years, has two claims to fame: he discovered the famous Siamese twins one day while crossing the Chao Phya River, and he built the first brick house of European design in the city. The twins left Thailand and went on to fame and fortune in the West, eventually ending their days in North Carolina. Hunter's house marked the beginning of an architectural revolution which would soon drastically transform the traditional capital founded by King Rama I in 1782.

The Chao Phya was the main street of early Bangkok, overlooked by the splendid mile-square Grand Palace and numerous Buddhist monasteries. Most commoners were compelled to live in floating houses moored by the hundreds along the banks, a rule that irked some of the foreign community, among them American missionaries, European diplomats, and traders like Hunter. At least one of the reasons for their discomfort was revealed in a memoir by F.A. Neale, another Englishman, who served with the Royal Siamese Navy in the same period:

Mr Hunter's floating house was double the size of any of the others, very neatly painted, and well-furnished, with a nice little verandah in front. The first night of my arrival I was dining there with all the English and Portuguese then assembled at Bangkok; we dined late,

The ruins of the palace of Constantine Phaulkon at Lopburi, dating from the late 17th century and showing early foreign influences.

by candlelight, and after dinner, walking up and down the verandah chatting about many little affairs, and the latest news, etc., I got so absorbed in the theme of the conversation as literally to forget that I was still upon the water; and taking one step too much, found myself all of a sudden up to my neck in water, with the tide running so strong, that I lost hold of one of the wooden pillars of the verandah; and though I am by no means a bad swimmer, I should inevitably have been drowned that night by being drawn right under the houses, if assistance had not come.

Perhaps there were other such mishaps in the course of convivial gatherings. Dr. Dan Beach Bradley, one of the American missionaries, hinted darkly in his journal about Hunter's "reputation as a tippler"; and if so, that may have been why Hunter finally used his influence in royal circles to gain permission for Europeans to build on solid ground. He himself was the first to take advantage of the ruling and put up what Neale described as "a very fine large prominent house, opposite to which the British ensign proudly floated on feast days and high days." A contemporary engraving shows it to have been a spacious, two-story affair with a verandah on the river, several solid-looking outbuildings which were probably servants' quarters, and a landing stage.

The rest of the foreigners soon followed. The Portuguese, who were the first of the Europeans to establish relations with Thailand during the Ayutthaya period, had already been granted a choice site by King Rama II for a "factory", or trading post. According to Neale, they originally planned "a splendid brick palace as a fit residence for their envoy at this illustrious court," but the ship bringing high-quality bricks as well as skilled masons from Goa was wrecked in a storm on the way. The first European legation to rise in the city, as a result, was "very indifferently constructed with bamboo, poles, lath and plaster, but it was an extensive house, cleanly white-washed, neatly furnished, and situated in one of the pleasantest positions in Siam." Some American missionaries settled nearby, their houses and the consulate forming a square in which grew a shady old tamarind tree of impressive size. Wrote Neale:

Under this tree Signor Marsinello de Rosa had constructed a few pretty garden seats, and reared a few choice flowers. And on this spot of a morning, before the sun's rays had waxed too warm, and of an evening after the heat of day had passed, the consul and his sedate neighbors used to assemble and discuss the latest news of the day, or watch the gay scene the river presented, or turn to the more gloomy themes and moralize on life and its many uncertain tenures.

As the 19th century progressed, a substantial number of other Western-style buildings joined these

Another view of Constantine Phaulkon's palace in Lopburi, showing European influence.

on both banks of the river. British, French, and American legations were established not far from the Portuguese, who gradually improved the building described by Neale and began turning it into the structure that still stands today. Dr. Bradley's Baptist Mission — a different group from those who enjoyed philosophical discussions under the tamarind tree with the Portuguese consul — lived in several uncomfortable places before they finally received permission to build on a site across the Chao Phya. "While we felt it right and suitable that we should have large and roomy dwellings," Dr. Bradley wrote, a bit waspishly, "we did not then feel justified in seeking nearly as expensive a finish on them as we had observed on the London Missionary Society dwellings in Penang and Singapore." The style decided on was typical of most foreign dwellings of the period, a few of which survive in the neighborhood:

Ours were made of wood, two tall stories high, covered with the common tiles of the country. They had verandahs all around them, with plank floors, ... and the rooms were all ceiled with rough boards whitewashed. The doors and windows especially were a great improvement on all their predecessors, being many and large, with posts plumb, and not leaning together or within, after the then universal custom of Siam, and the upper part of the window shutters were made of a coarse kind of Venetian blinds.

Having been rescued from the inconveniences of floating houses, the Europeans discovered a new one on land: the lack of proper roads along which they could enjoy an evening stroll or a carriage ride. Once more they turned for assistance to the ruler, who by this time was the remarkable King Mongkut, or Rama IV. Already committed to modernizing his kingdom — he put up the first Western buildings in the Grand Palace compound (one of them inspired by London's Big Ben) and hired an Englishwoman named Anna Leonowens to teach some of his children — the king was sympathetic to the complaint and initiated a road-building program.

One of the thoroughfares that resulted was Charoen Krung, known to the foreign colony as New Road, which ran along the river just behind the legations all the way to the Chinese quarter. The latter was by then a densely populated area, thanks to a flood of Chinese immigrants, and solid buildings of brick and mortar were appearing there, too, as well as across the river where many of the larger godowns were located. By the end of Mongkut's reign, Charoen Krung and the lanes leading off it were lined with shophouses, small hotels, and various other establishments and was Bangkok's acknowledged center of commerce and foreign architecture.

The transformation of the city increased rapidly under Mongkut's son, King Chulalongkorn, the first Thai monarch to travel abroad and as dedicated as his

Robert Hunter's house on the Chao Phya, reputedly the first brick dwelling built by a foreigner in Bangkok. From Narrative of a Residence in Siam *(1850) by F.A. Neale.*

father to the idea of modernization. An early trip was to Penang, Singapore, and Java, where the king was sufficiently impressed by the splendor of British and Dutch colonial buildings to emulate some of them within the Grand Palace as well as nearby. Foreign architects, mainly Italian and British, were called on to execute the designs, which generally reflected those popular in Europe at the time — massive structures with domes, Romanesque facades, and elaborate masonry — though sometimes with an unexpected touch of Thai style.

The Chakri Throne Hall, for instance, the first major addition to the Grand Palace compound since its founding, was planned by its British designer as a wholly European building surmounted by three domes. During construction, the king decided to replace the domes with Thai-style spires, resulting in a hybrid that managed to proclaim its progressive spirit while still harmonizing with the classic structures surrounding it. Behind the Throne Hall was the Inner Palace, closed to most outsiders and inhabited solely by young boys below the age of puberty and women: queens, concubines, attendants, and unmarried princesses from former reigns, who were forbidden to leave the palace compound. Here, too, in a center of traditional beliefs, there was a new enthusiasm for Western-style residences with pillared verandahs, airy rooftop terraces, spiral staircases, and occasional whimsical touches like false chimneys.

In 1884, an ambitious, 32-year-old Dane named H.N. Andersen bought a small hotel on the river called the Oriental, which catered mostly to visiting seamen. Andersen believed the time had come for Bangkok to have a proper hotel, as opposed to the rather rowdy establishments that then went by the name, and to this end he hired an Italian architect to come up with something to rival those of neighboring ports like Singapore and Penang. The new Oriental opened three years later, with an imposing facade on the Chao Phya, public rooms that boasted Brussels carpets, French wall paper, and couches upholstered in peacock-blue velvet, and a restaurant presided over by a chef named Troisoeufs, who had formerly been in charge of the kitchen at the French legation.

By the early years of the present century, few Thais of means lived in a traditional house, especially in Bangkok and provincial capitals like Chiang Mai. The leading fashion was for multi-storied Victorian structures of often complex design and decoration: turrets and oddly-shaped windows, widow's walks, capacious verandahs, stained glass, and a lavish application of intricately carved fretwork. Royal palaces, appropriately, were the most elaborate. One, known as Vimarn Mek, was built by Chulalongkorn near the end of his rule and is reputed to be the largest teak dwelling in the world, a honey-colored creation overlooking a pond of deep jade-green. Phya Thai Palace, where the king's principal queen moved after

The Portuguese Consulate and missionary houses in Bangkok in the 1840's. From Narrative of a Residence in Siam *(1850) by F.A. Neale.*

his death, had a five-storey tower with verandahs on two floors and a large open audience hall that could seat up to 500 people. When it was turned into a deluxe hotel for a brief period in the late 1920's, tea dances were held in the hall and guests were treated to performances of Thai classical dance in a Greek pavilion in the garden. The greatest concentration of such buildings was to found in the Dusit District, the most fashionable residential area for members of the royal family, but as the city expanded and roads began to lead away from the old center, others rose in what were formerly regarded as the distant suburbs.

The simpler bungalow style described by Dr. Bradley was popular with foreign residents of the capital, as well as among the teak wallahs who were settling in Chiang Mai, then a journey of several weeks from Bangkok by boat and elephant back. These were sizeable houses, often raised on columns, with deep, cool verandahs, large rooms, and French windows looking over equally spacious gardens; in the sleeping quarters the bed was often placed in the center and surrounded by what was called a "mosquito house," amounting to a little room made of mesh. The kitchen was usually separate, as were quarters to accomodate the numerous servants who took care of the compound and its residents.

Other styles, too, appeared on the scene in the reign of Chulalongkorn's Oxford-educated successor, King Vajiravudh, who built a number of houses that resembled Swiss chalets, Tudor cottages, and a curious but effective blend of Gothic and Moorish; one of the latter currently serves as the office of the Prime Minister. The British Embassy shocked some but showed prescience by moving to a new location far from the river, where it assumed residence in a group of solid whitewashed brick buildings containing huge rooms with high ceilings, similar to many colonial edifices throughout the Empire. The property was acquired from a prosperous merchant named Nai Lert, who even before there were roads leading out to the district had laid out a park on the bank of Klong San Saeb and built a large, multi-roofed weekend home of Burmese inspiration, almost without walls except for the bedrooms.

Different from one another as these foreign-style dwellings were in appearance, whimsical as some of them seem in today's context with their ornate and elaborate architectural flourishes, most shared an important characteristic. They were built for life in a tropical climate in the days before airconditioning. Keeping cool was a major consideration, and it was usually achieved through lofty rooms, verandahs, numerous doors and windows, vast gardens with lily-filled ponds and shady flamboyants, tamarinds, and rain trees. In this sense they can be seen as natural successors to the traditional Thai house, which had met a similar need with its raised platform and living quarters arranged to catch every available breeze.

WESTERN-INSPIRED

The structures shown on these pages are a small sample of those built by Thai royalty in the late 19th and early 20th centuries following Western models. Inspired by both travel and photographs of European capitals, they encompass a variety of forms, from neo-Gothic to Victorian folly, though most shared a common characteristic of airy lightness appropriate to the tropical climate.

LEFT: *Interior of Government House, originally built in the early 20th century for a member of King Rama VI's court. The European statues and blend of Western architectural styles are characteristic of the period.*

BELOW: *A performance of Thai classic dance, given in a Greek temple on the grounds of Phya Thai Palace during the brief period when it served as a hotel in the late 1920's; from a guidebook to Bangkok published by the Royal State Railways, which operated the hotel.*

RIGHT: *Some royally-built pavilions from the turn of the century. These structures no longer exist and their location is uncertain.*

RIGHT: *The audience hall of the former Phya Thai palace, today the Phra Mongkut Military Hospital. It was built by King Chulalongkorn (Rama V), and after his death his widowed Queen lived there until her own in 1919. Tea dances were held in the hall when the palace was opened as a hotel.*

VIMARN MEK

Vimarn Mek was designed by a son of King Chulalongkorn. The original plan was to build the palace on the island of Si Chang, in the Gulf of Thailand, but the incomplete structure was moved to Bangkok's Dusit District, not far from a Western-style Throne Hall in 1900. The king lived in Vimarn Mek for a few years before moving to Dusit Palace, after which it served as the residence of several royal ladies until his death in 1910. The palace was restored by Her Majesty Queen Sirikit as part of the celebration of Bangkok's Bicentennial in 1982 and is now open to the public.

Built entirely of teak — supposedly the largest teak structure in the world — Vimarn Mek is a rambling collection of interconnected rooms, with spiral staircases leading to the upper floors. The top floor was reserved for the king and contains an imported weighing machine, a large copper bath, and the first shower ever seen in Thailand.

FAR LEFT: *View of the exterior.*
LEFT AND RIGHT: *Some of the public rooms in Vimarn Mek. The palace was largely empty when Queen Sirikit set about the task of restoring it, and she drew upon the royal family's large collection of furniture and decorative items to accurately reflect the period in which it was built. Most of these were European, though some were especially ordered to meet Thai tastes of the time. Old photographs of King Chulalongkorn and his family are hung on the walls.*

LEFT: *Exterior view of Vimarn Mek's octagonal structure.*

RIGHT ABOVE: *The Throne Hall, with seats bearing the royal insignia; on the wall behind hangs a portrait of King Chulalongkorn.*

RIGHT BELOW: *The King's study, furnished with a variety of items acquired on his trips to European capitals during his long reign.*

DIPLOMATIC TIES

The Portuguese were the first Europeans to establish contact with Thailand, in 1511 during the Ayutthaya period, and their embassy is also the oldest in Bangkok. The architectural development of the present building is uncertain, but the land on which it stands was granted to the first consul in 1820 by order of King Rama II.

A "factory", or trading station, was built first which now houses the embassy offices. According to one source, the original consular residence was a simple structure and was later replaced when better building materials became available, probably in the mid-19th century. It faces the river, as most buildings did in those days, and the upper rooms with an airy verandah extending along the front appear to have been added to the thick-walled lower section. The floor of the top half consists of fine teak planks of exceptional width.

ABOVE: *The exterior of the residence.*
LEFT: *Tiled porch off the ground floor of the residence, leading to a garden and the river.*
RIGHT: *Upstairs verandah overlooking the garden, which has been left unairconditioned. The two old chairs in the foreground are teak, while the groups in the background are rattan, with cushions covered in local cotton; the pillows with the royal white elephant are Thai silk.*

SPACIOUS QUARTERS

During the first half of Bangkok's history, all the foreign legations were located on or near the busy Chao Phya River, making it easy for representatives to go up by launch on official business to the Grand Palace. The French Embassy residence is the second oldest remaining today, built in the middle of the 19th century and gradually added to over the years. The building faces the river, with a lawn leading down to the water, and in the style of the day had a broad verandah and living quarters on the upper floor, affording maximum air circulation as well as protection against floods.

Also shown on these pages are details of several other houses in the neighborhood of the embassy, which was then regarded as a prime residential site for Europeans. The houses are elaborately decorated with Victorian fretwork and follow the same general architectural style as the French residence.

LEFT ABOVE: *Exterior of the French embassy residence, shaded by a large flame tree; the fretwork decoration was used on most wooden houses built in Bangkok during the 19th century.*
LEFT BELOW: *The dining room of the embassy, which overlooks the Chao Phya River.*
RIGHT: *Decorative details on several old houses in the vicinity of the embassy; all are wood except for the wrought iron balustrades on the lower right.*

ON THE VERANDAH

The rented home of Anne and Tom Tofield was built around 1910 on upper Sathorn Road, an area then just becoming popular for residential purposes, especially among Bangkok's foreign community, even though it was far from the commercial center along the river. Large rooms and breezy verandahs overlooking cool gardens were a characteristic of nearly all the European-style houses built during this period. Many have now been airconditioned and some, like this one, stand in the shadow of modern office buildings; but they still preserve the old sense of spacious and tropical living in the center of the city.

ABOVE, LEFT AND RIGHT: *Views of the verandah of the Tofield house. Rattan furniture and numerous potted plants add to the feeling of airy coolness.*

AN OLD HOUSE IN DHONBURI

The house shown on these pages is of unknown architectural origins, and was built around the middle of the 19th century, probably by a European in service to the Thai monarchy. It is located on Klong Mon in Dhonburi, across the river from Bangkok, which served briefly as the capital after the destruction of Ayutthaya. Many foreigners lived in Dhonburi during the early Bangkok period.

The house was apparently modified a number of times over the years. An airy, multi-windowed sitting room with louvered shutters was added to the upper portion, and arched doorways on the ground floor were altered so that they became rectangular.

RIGHT AND FAR RIGHT: *Views of the upstairs sitting room; the furniture consists of reproductions by Pure Design, using samples of woodcarving from an old Thai bed, for example, to create the desk. Lowered shutters allow a free circulation of air in the room.*

LEFT ABOVE: *Upstairs room overlooking Klong Mon. The jars are Khmer and the bronze rain drum is from Laos; elephant howdahs inspired the design of the chairs.*
LEFT BELOW: *The ground floor, tiled in marble, and a breezeway linking two parts of the upper floor; the wicker furniture is from Pure Design.*

ABOVE: *Exterior of the old part of the house, showing a royal seal on the gable board; the furniture in the garden is a reproduction of turn-of-the-century wickerwork.*
LEFT: *Front of the house facing the klong.*

HISTORIC CONNECTIONS

The roomy, all-teak Chiang Mai house shown on these pages is of unusual historical interest, having been built by Louis T. Leonowens, son of the famous Anna who was brought by King Rama IV to teach some of his royal children. Louis later returned to Thailand and, granted some timber concessions by King Rama V (one of Anna's pupils), lived for a time in the north.

The actual date of construction is uncertain, but it originally stood on the west side of the Ping River and was moved to its present site on the east side by Leonowens before 1876. Following his brief stay there, it was the home of a Borneo Company manager until 1927 when another Borneo manager, W. Bain, took up residence. When Bain retired in 1938 he bought the compound, which contains several other buildings, and lived there with his Thai wife and family until his death in 1958. The family still owns the property, which is known locally as the Bain Compound.

LEFT ABOVE: *A lavish use of pierced woodcarvings adds to the airy quality of the interior, as seen here in the main sitting area with its views of the garden. The furniture is locally made rattan.*
LEFT BELOW: *Entrance stairway, showing the gingerbread fretwork which was typical of many houses of the period.*
RIGHT: *View of the house from the garden, which contains a large flame tree.*

IN A SPACIOUS GARDEN

Khunying Lurasakdi Sampatisiri's unusual house, occupying one of Bangkok's largest private compounds, was built around the turn of the century by her father, a businessman named Nai Lert. A pavilion-like structure with layered roofs, somewhat reminiscent of Burmese architecture, it was originally intended to be a weekend house, accessible only by a nearby canal. When Nai Lert and his family moved there full time, more partitions were added to form rooms; in recent years, Khunying Lurasakdi has glassed in other areas so that airconditioning could be installed while retaining the garden views that contribute so much to the beauty of the house.

The garden, which includes an extensive orchid house, is noted for its wide variety of tropical plants, many of which were used by Khunying Lurasakdi when she planted the compound of the Hilton International Hotel on a neighbouring site.

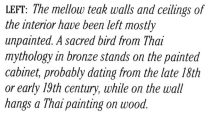

LEFT: *The mellow teak walls and ceilings of the interior have been left mostly unpainted. A sacred bird from Thai mythology in bronze stands on the painted cabinet, probably dating from the late 18th or early 19th century, while on the wall hangs a Thai painting on wood.*

ABOVE AND LEFT: *One section of the spacious interior, formerly open, has been airconditioned, though the large sheets of glass allow an uninterrupted view of the garden outside. The furniture is covered with Thai silk, while Thai and Chinese porcelains provide additional accents of color. The sofas and chairs on the left were inspired by elephant howdahs.*

LEFT: *View of the house and entrance drive. The multi-layered roofs, reminiscent of Burmese architecture, have vents in between them; as the hot air rises and escapes this creates a natural circulation which keeps the interior unusually cool.*

LEFT BELOW: *A selection of the extensive garden of Nai Lert Park, in which antique jars, some planted with water lilies, are placed amid the lush greenery; partially screened by this planting is a swimming pool.*

ABOVE: *Some of the numerous orchids continually in bloom in the nursery area, providing a regular supply of cut flowers for the house.*

RIGHT: *View of the entrance drive from the house. The shrubs cut in topiary shapes are characteristic of traditional Thai gardens. Royal palms and hybrid bougainvillea trained to grow as shrubs line the drive, while in the background can be seen a Thai-style pavilion.*

THE ORIENTAL

One of Bangkok's landmarks, the Oriental Hotel was built on the site of an older structure bearing the same name and opened for business in 1887. The original hotel faced the river and consisted of a central building with opulently furnished public rooms and long wings that contained the guest rooms. A few years after its opening, King Chulalongkorn (Rama V) himself came down by royal launch from the Grand Palace to view its much-discussed amenities.

The hotel has been modified a number of times, particularly since the second world war, with the addition of two new wings in modern style. The oldest remaining section, called the Author's Wing, contains suites decorated in traditional styles and named after noted writers who have stayed at the hotel, as well as a lobby that preserves the atmosphere of the late 19th century even though it is largely the work of contemporary designers.

LEFT: *Part of the Author's Lounge, in the oldest part of the Oriental, preserves a 19th-century charm through period furnishings. The painting shows the hotel as it looked shortly after its opening in 1887.*
RIGHT ABOVE: *The Author's Lounge, where afternoon tea is served.*
RIGHT BELOW: *Several of the hotel's choicest suites are located in this wing, among them the Noel Coward Suite, with silk wall covering decorated in traditional Thai designs. Other writers honored by suites in the hotel include Joseph Conrad, Somerset Maugham, James Michener, Graham Greene, and Barbara Cartland.*

TROPICAL MODERN

There is a new housing project, in the center of Bangkok, offering what it claims to be the only Gothic-style town houses available in Thailand. This distinction, however, is likely to be short-lived: if Gothic proves popular, similar projects are sure to rise and cash in on the latest of a long list of architectural fads that includes Spanish, Tudor, Swiss chalet, and something faintly French that goes by the name of Louis. Waiting in the wings is "Castle Style," complete with moat and drawbridge leading into the estate, a sample of which is under construction as this is being written.

Serious Thai architects, understandably, take a dim view of these whimsical creations, just as they do of the box-like rowshops that line most urban streets and give them an appearance of drab conformity. They see them as showing a lack of imagination, not to mention taste, and there is no denying that a drive through the newer residential areas of Bangkok offers few pleasures for anyone in search of real architectural flair. Even when the residents are not peering through stained-glass windows or from Cinderella turrets, they are likely to be living in houses that seem to have little to do with the country in which they are located.

Yet despite this tendency to import Western models without regard for their suitability, the situation is not as hopeless as it might appear. Thailand today does have talented architects and

LEFT: *The contemporary home of Manop Charoensuk and Islay Lyons is set in a lush yet compact garden which has been divided into sections to give the impression of occupying more space than it actually does.*

A nine-sided pavilion designed by M.L. Tri Devakul. Right: The Phuket Yacht Club combines modern architectural techniques with a feeling for traditional forms.

interior designers, and their work is being increasingly appreciated by clients who want something other than a mere oddity. Moreover, especially in domestic architecture, many of them are demonstrating that it is possible to blend traditional concepts with modern materials and methods of construction to produce styles that can still be confidently proclaimed as Thai.

Several of the architects, for instance, have derived inspiration from the classic cluster house, in which several structures are arranged on a common platform, and come up with variations that appear to suit current life styles as much as the originals did those of rural families. Others have managed to design contemporary homes in which expanses of glass, high ceilings, and flower-filled patios achieve the spacious open quality of the past even in urban surroundings. Outside the city, in places like Phuket and Chiang Mai, natural scenery has been made an integral part of the total design concept.

This effort to use native architectural and decorative elements in their work is not confined to homes. New hotels and office buildings, too, frequently display prominent features — layered roofs, for example, and a lavish use of mellow-toned wood — that give them a distinction notably lacking in the glass-and-cement boxes of only a decade or so ago.

Landscape gardeners are making maximum use of limited space and taking advantage of Thailand's tropical climate to create luxuriant vistas as re-

freshing as those once enjoyed from bungalow verandahs. In this they are aided by the vast number of ornamental plants and trees that have been introduced into the country in recent years, bringing far more color and variety to Thai gardens.

Perhaps the most visible manifestations of a growing appreciation for things Thai can be found in the field of interior decoration. As a glimpse through almost any of the numerous local magazines devoted to homes will reveal, designers are finding imaginative ways to employ Thailand's rich range of traditional crafts, in settings that please and often enchant. The lustrous, handwoven silks and supple cottons of the country — regarded as inferior to foreign textiles not very long ago — are now commonly seen on cushions, upholstery, wall coverings, draperies, and in a dozen other places in the home. An ornate piece of antique wood-carving, a faded old painting on cloth, an elegant lacquered chest with gold-and-black designs, a strikingly illuminated shelf of 13th-century bowls from Sukhothai, bring both beauty and drama to an otherwise modern setting. Even the plain but elegant pots and baskets and simple furniture of village life, new as well as old, are being lovingly refinished to enhance sophisticated city households.

Through the work of such talented people, a new and striking style has evolved, one as unmistakably Thai as the fabulous temples and elegant houses that once gave the kingdom its distinctive quality.

CONTEMPORARY CLUSTER HOUSE

The home of Manop Charoensuk and Islay Lyons was designed by John Rifenberg, a Bangkok-based architect whose firm has been responsible for many of Thailand's fine contemporary residences. Employing the concept of the classic cluster house, it consists of three structures around a central wooden deck: a large, rectangular living room which occupies an entire side and two bedroom units on the right and left sides. A covered walkway allows passage between the units in rainy weather and also provides an open-air sitting area. The garden of the house has been divided into sections to give the impression of occupying far more space than it actually does.

LEFT ABOVE: *Just below the deck, an area paved with laterite slabs is sheltered by a trellis on which are grown several flowering vines.*
LEFT: *A wooden spirit house, ornately carved to resemble a palace, is an attractive feature in the garden.*

ABOVE: *A small pool, faced with laterite and planted with both day and night blooming water lilies, dominates the side garden; crotons provide splashes of colorful foliage in the greenery.*

LEFT: *A stone Khmer lion stands beside the boldly-patterned leaves of a Sanchezia shrub.*

ABOVE: *The central deck of the house, where a sitting area is provided under the covered walkway that connects the three structures. At the base of a large raintree shading the deck stands a glazed Chinese figure; the cushions on the rattan chairs are covered with handwoven Chiang Mai cotton.*

ABOVE: *The living room, forming one side of the deck. The leather-cushioned chairs were designed by M.L. Thaodeva Devakul, and the bronze figures on the table behind the sofa are 18th century Burmese; an elephant howdah has been put to use as a bar on the left.*

LIVING WITH ANTIQUES

When Police Lt. Col. Sprung Ulapathorn and his wife Khun Anongnart acquired their home in a Bangkok housing estate, it was much smaller than it is today. Over the years it has been enlarged and modified several times, acquiring both spacious rooms and a distinctive style. Khun Anongnart, the owner of an antique shop, is also an enthusiastic collector of art objects, and the house is richly furnished with items from a variety of cultures, ranging from Thai to Tibetan.

ABOVE: *The living room; the rug hanging on the far wall is from Tibet, while the bronze rain-drum in the foreground is Laotian.*
FAR LEFT: *Another view of the living room, dominated by a large carved Thai bed and a Chinese lacquer screen. Elsewhere can be seen Burmese Buddha images, lacquer-coated priests from Burma and a 12th-century stone figure from Cambodia.*
LEFT: *Burmese priests and Buddha images with a manuscript cabinet.*

179

ABOVE: *The dining room; a pair of carved wooden Burmese window panels, dating from the 18th century, hang on the wall on the left, while two standing figures, also from Burma, are displayed on the cabinet to the right of the table. The lighting fixtures, still being made today, were often found in old Thai houses and temples.*
RIGHT: *A place setting, showing a Chinese fish plate, Thai cotton place-mat and runner, and a typical Thai flower arrangement of folded lotus blossoms.*

RIGHT ABOVE: *Carved wooden chairs with ivory decorations, a red lacquer* kantok *table from northern Thailand, a 12th-century stone figure of Uma, and a Thai display cabinet form a grouping in front of wall panels from an old Chinese house.*

RIGHT BELOW: *On a carved Thai table are displayed a Burmese covered box in red lacquer, a seated wooden figure from Burma, boxes of northern Thai workmanship, and an old embroidered piece of cloth from northeastern Thailand; the tops of pillars carved in the shape of lotus flowers form bases for the lamps.*

ABOVE AND RIGHT: *Stone figures, both old and new, add to the appeal of the garden. The one on the left above is Khmer, while those in the other pictures are Chinese.*

ABOVE: *View of the garden; a gilded wooden gable from an old northern temple is used on the pavilion at right, and on the lawn are displayed old Thai water jars in varying shapes and sizes and carved columns. The orchids are growing on old coconut palm trunks.*

FRESH LOOK FOR A COURTYARD HOUSE

A foreign couple who have lived in Thailand for many years built their home in a housing estate in suburban Bangkok. Because the piece of land was relatively small, they decided to arrange the rooms around an inner garden-court, with the main doors opening onto a covered gallery; thus maximum use was made of the property while also ensuring privacy. An American designer, Michael Bertolini, was called on to help with the interior decoration, which includes both European furniture and a large collection of Asian art; a Bangkok furniture maker, Khun Prinya, was responsible for executing most of the designs. Plants chosen for the lush central garden were limited to varieties with blue and white flowers, and Chinese jars in the same colors are used as planters around the tiled gallery.

LEFT ABOVE: *View of the tiled gallery, just outside the living room; an old Thai woodcarving hangs on the wall above the rattan and cane sofa. The coffee table is made from a wooden lintel from Chiang Mai, protected by glass.*
LEFT BELOW: *Another section of the gallery, which occupies three sides of the central garden, glimpsed on the left. On the wall above an old Chinese altar table hang two galae from northern Thai houses. Some of the glazed ceramic plant containers are old, while others are replicas made not far from Bangkok in Rajburi.*
RIGHT: *The library; old lacquered Chinese doors conceal a television set. The fan on the rosewood and marble table is also Chinese and made of silver.*

BELOW: *A wooden Burmese Buddha image, covered in gilt lacquer.*
LEFT: *The living room; on the left wall hangs an unusually large Coramandel screen, while on the right is a Burmese* kalaga *cloth thickly embroidered with gold thread and imitation gems. Thai silk is used for upholstery and cushions.*

DECORATING WITH SILK

The home of Gerald Pierce, head designer for the Jim Thompson Thai Silk Company, dates from the 1920's when the airy bungalow style was still favored by many residents of Bangkok. Several years ago it was moved from its original location and reconstructed elsewhere in the city, preserving its spaciousness but with added amenities like airconditioning and modern bathrooms.

Mr. Pierce's interest in fabrics and antiques is apparent throughout the house in his decorations, which include silk-covered walls and cushions, prehistoric pottery, old woodcarvings, and reproductions of traditional Thai furniture.

LEFT ABOVE: *The dining room. A replica of a Khmer head stands on an old cabinet decorated with gold and black lacquer. The walls are covered with Thai silk.*
LEFT: *The master bedroom. The mirror is made from two pieces of carved Burmese wood, and a painting from India hangs above an old captain's chest on the right.*
RIGHT: *Red lacquer container from Chiang Mai against a background of printed Thai silk in the dining room.*

ABOVE AND RIGHT: *One of the two living rooms in the house, with a view of the garden below. The far wall is of bleached pinewood, and a clay pot of the Ayutthaya period stands before it. A collection of ivory bracelets is displayed in a bowl on the Thai bed that serves as a coffee table.*

ABOVE: *Another sitting area, with silk-covered furniture and a teak coffee table with Chinese carvings; the straw matting on the floor is locally made.*
LEFT: *Thai silk cushions.*

PHUKET BEACH HOUSE

M.L. Tri Devakul, one of Thailand's fore-most architects, has designed a number of hotel projects on the southern island of Phuket, among them the Phuket Yacht Club and the Phuket Meridien. His own house is on a hill between Kata Yai and Kata Noi beaches with a sweeping view of the Andaman Sea.

The complex consists of a large main residence, built on a series of levels down the hillside, a dining pavilion, and a number of out-buildings around a terraced garden; a salt-water swimming pool incorporating natural boul-ders in its design overlooks the sea at the lowest level. Steep roofs and lofty ceilings are a notable feature of the residence, as is the use of sugar-palm trunks as verandah pillars; a fine woodcarving from a northern temple forms the gable in the master bedroom. Airconditioning makes it possible to use the house even during the strong winds of Phuket's monsoon season.

PRECEDING PAGES: *Views of the swimming pool and garden, showing the overlapping roofs of the main house and the thatched-roof dining pavilion.*

LEFT: *Living room of main house, which overlooks the sea; paintings by Thai artists hang on the wall, and heavy Thai cotton is used on the locally-made furniture.*

ABOVE: *A large bronze Buddha image in a raised alcove faces the sea.*

RIGHT: *The dining pavilion, hung with large wooden trays from northern Thailand, used in preparing and serving food. Old wormwood boards, salvaged from logs found washed up on Phuket beaches, have been used for walls in the rear; the thatched walls on the left can be lowered during the monsoon season.*

Some examples of the *galae* decorations found on northern-style houses in Chiang Mai. The exact significance of these is unknown, particularly in more elaborately carved versions like these, but designs often include the traditional flame motif.

THE CENTRAL PLAINS
SMALL FAMILY HOUSE

The traditional central plains house, made in prefabricated sections, is raised on sturdy pillars and has walls that slant slightly inward, steep tiled or thatched roofs with broad over-hangs, and bargeboards with curving ends. A typically small-family dwelling has a sleeping room opening onto a covered veran-dah and an open platform where most social activities take place; the kitchen is housed in a separate unit. The area below the house is used to keep the family animals and, in some, for weaving and other handicrafts.

1. TERRACE
2. VERANDAH
3. BEDROOM
4. KITCHEN

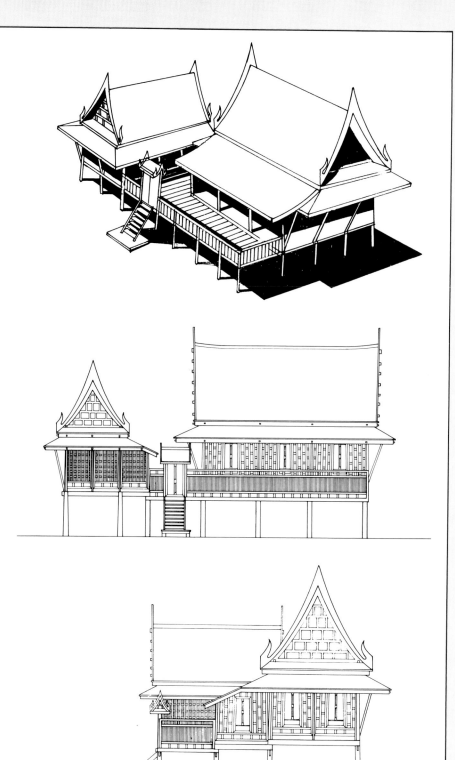

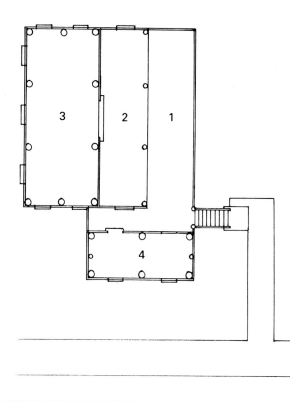

THE CENTRAL PLAINS CLUSTER HOUSE

The cluster-type house evolved to meet the needs of extended families, who could not be comfortably accommodated in the smaller structures. Several separate sleeping rooms, each with a covered verandah, are arranged around the raised platform, which then serves as a common meeting place; all share the same kitchen and bath facilities. An entrance pavilion where guests are received is often located at the front of the house, at the top of the open staircase. This type of house is subject to numerous variations.

1. ENTRANCE PORCH
2. TERRACE
3. VERANDAH
4. BEDROOM
5. KITCHEN
6. FRONT LIVING AREA
7. FAMILY AREA
8. TOILET
9. BATH AREA

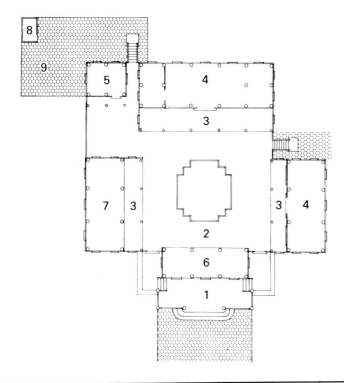

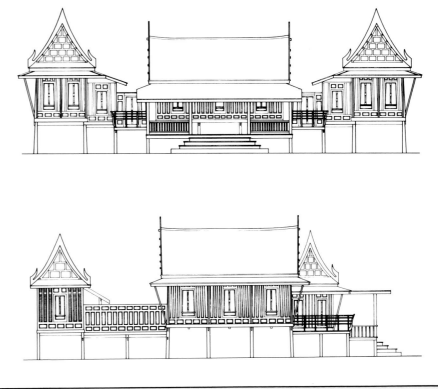

THE NORTHERN THAI HOUSE

Traditional northern-style houses usually have walls that lean outward toward the roof and smaller windows than those of the Central Region; sleeping rooms are sometimes arranged on either side of a corridor as in the example shown here. Decoratively-carved pieces of wood that some have found reminiscent of buffalo horns adorn the roof of the better houses, particularly in the Chiang Mai area. The entire structure is raised on pillars and has an open platform in the front. Shown on this page is the small family house and opposite is an example of the cluster house.

1. TERRACE
2. VERANDAH
3. BEDROOM
4. KITCHEN
5. STORAGE
6. GRANARY
7. WATER SUPPLY SHELF

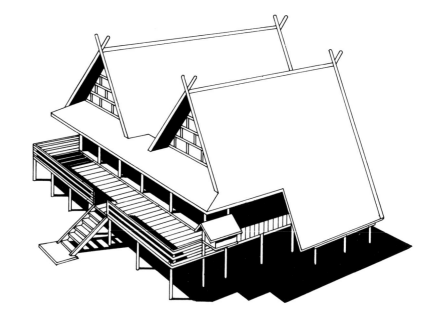

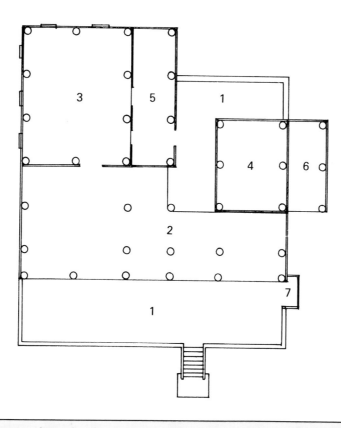

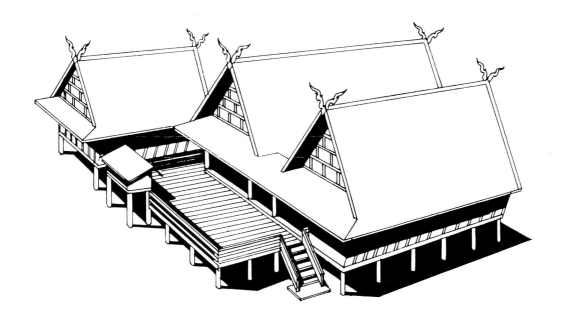

1. TERRACE
2. VERANDAH
3. BEDROOM
4. KITCHEN
5. WATER SUPPLY SHELF

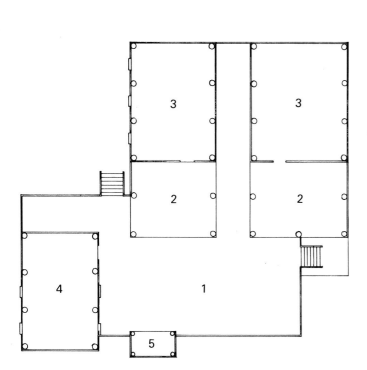

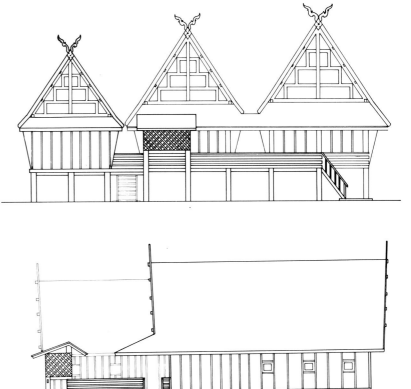

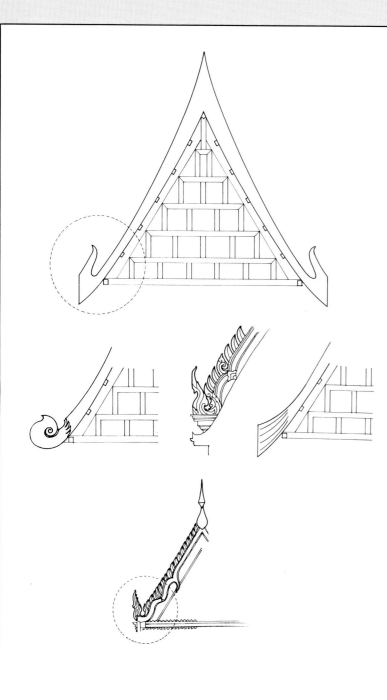

The bargeboards (*pan-lom*) on the traditional Central Thai house have a decorative feature at the end known as *ngao*. This can take many forms, as these examples show, and probably evolved from Khmer temple architecture.

Entrance to a traditional house, at the top of the stairway leading to the central platform, covered with a Thai roof; a lock for securing the door can be seen on the raised threshold.

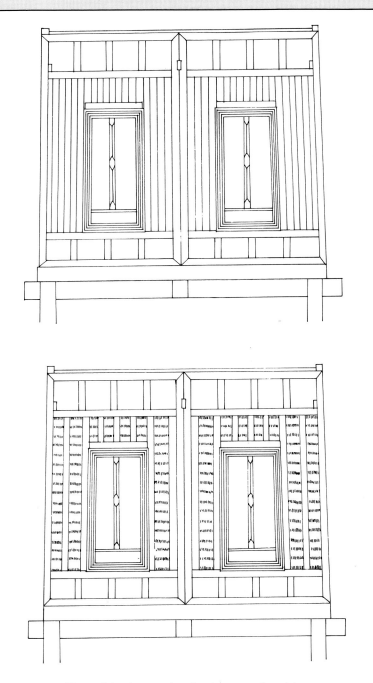

Examples of paneling on a traditional house, of an elaborate type found in more prosperous homes. Such paneling appears to have been a fairly late development and was a way of using left-over pieces of wood.

The wall in the top drawing is a type found in more common houses, where fancy paneling was not used. Below is the wall of a kitchen, with spaces between the boards to allow for more ventilation.

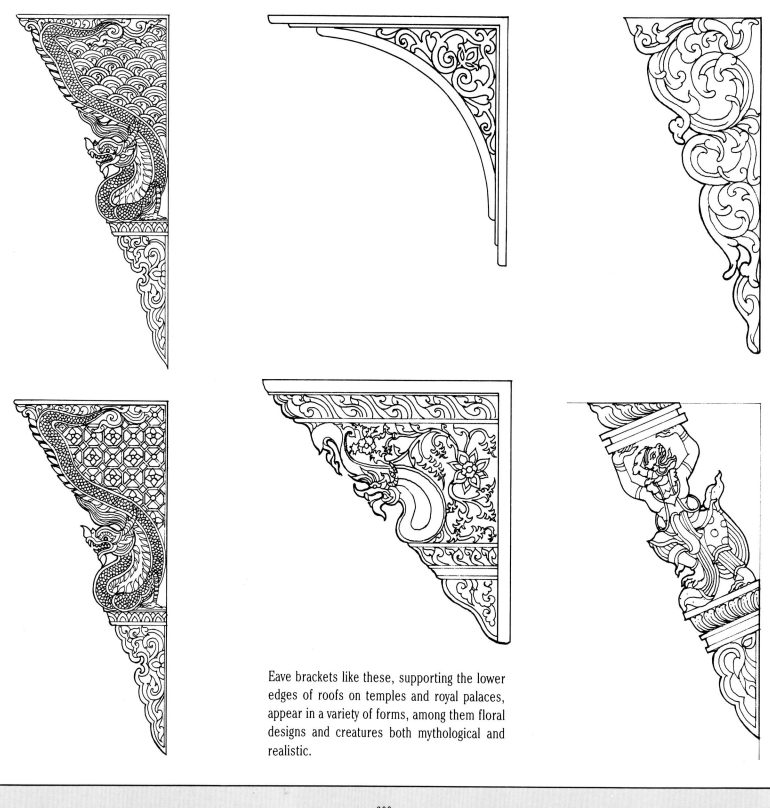

Eave brackets like these, supporting the lower edges of roofs on temples and royal palaces, appear in a variety of forms, among them floral designs and creatures both mythological and realistic.

These drawings are examples of designs for *ham yon*, carved wooden lintels placed above the doorway leading into the inner room of a northern house; the symbolic significance of the designs is uncertain, though most of them appeared on numerous houses.

More examples of the northern *ham yons*, which are believed to protect the owner of the house from evil spirits. The size was determined by measuring the owner's foot, a small lintel being three times as long and a large one four times as long.

Samples of fretwork balcony decorations produced sometimes by hand, sometimes by machine; these became popular in the 19th century and are found on many buildings of the period. The designs are often traditional Thai or Chinese.

Examples of ornamental strips of fretwork used along the eaves of houses, especially in the 19th and early 20th century. Many of the designs reflect traditional Thai motifs.

精美日

The entrance of an old Chinese shophouse and windows typical of 19th century western-style houses with louvered shutters and fanlights.

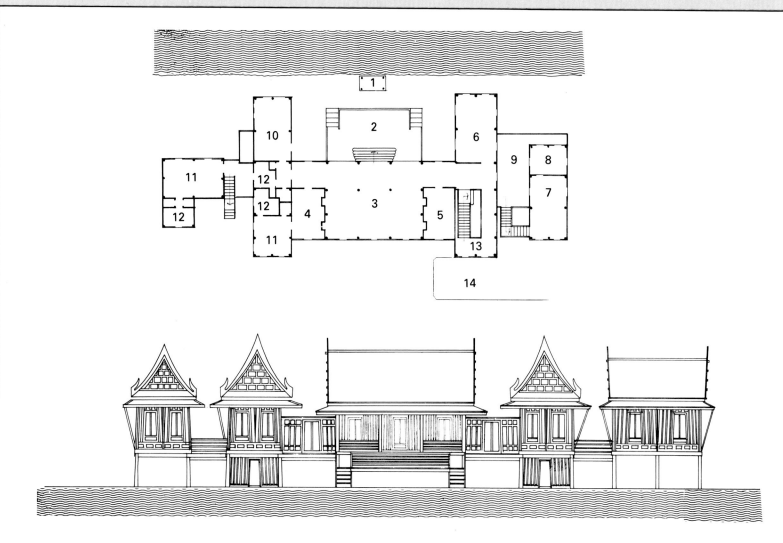

JIM THOMPSON HOUSE

Architecturally, the Jim Thompson house (pictured on pages 86-91) faces Klong Maha Nag and by tradition guests would have arrived via the *sala* on the canal. This being impractical in modern Bangkok, entrance is through a stairhall at the back. The kitchen and pantry were formed by one of the old houses, while others of varying size were used for the living room, the guest room and study, and the master bedroom, all joined together in a non-traditional way.

1. SALA (PAVILION) ON CANAL
2. TERRACE
3. LIVING ROOM
4. STUDY
5. PORCELAIN DISPLAY ROOM
6. DINING ROOM
7. KITCHEN
8. PANTRY
9. PASSAGEWAY
10. MASTER BEDROOM
11. GUEST ROOM
12. BATHROOM
13. ENTRANCE STAIRHALL
14. COURTYARD

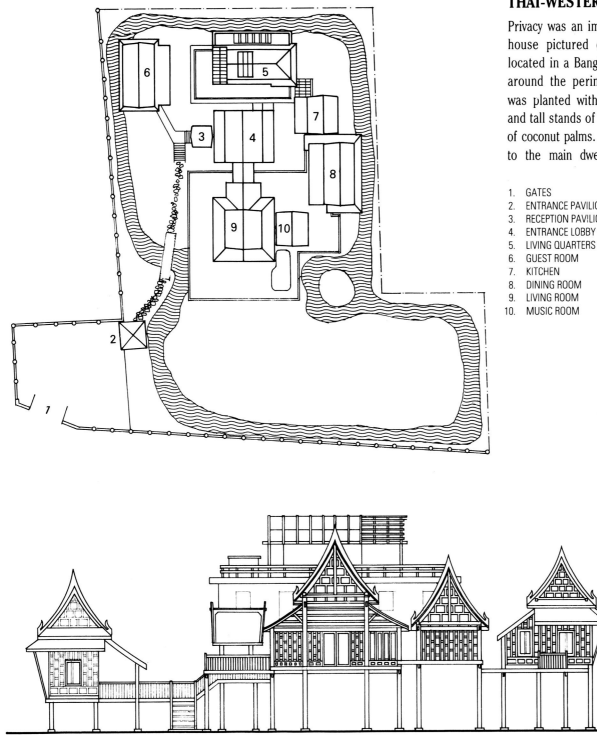

THAI-WESTERN COMPROMISE

Privacy was an important consideration in the house pictured on pages 112-119, which is located in a Bangkok suburb. A canal was dug around the perimeter of the propety, which was planted with fruit and ornamental trees and tall stands of bamboo, as well as a number of coconut palms. The guest room is connected to the main dwelling by a wooden walkway.

1. GATES
2. ENTRANCE PAVILION
3. RECEPTION PAVILION
4. ENTRANCE LOBBY
5. LIVING QUARTERS
6. GUEST ROOM
7. KITCHEN
8. DINING ROOM
9. LIVING ROOM
10. MUSIC ROOM

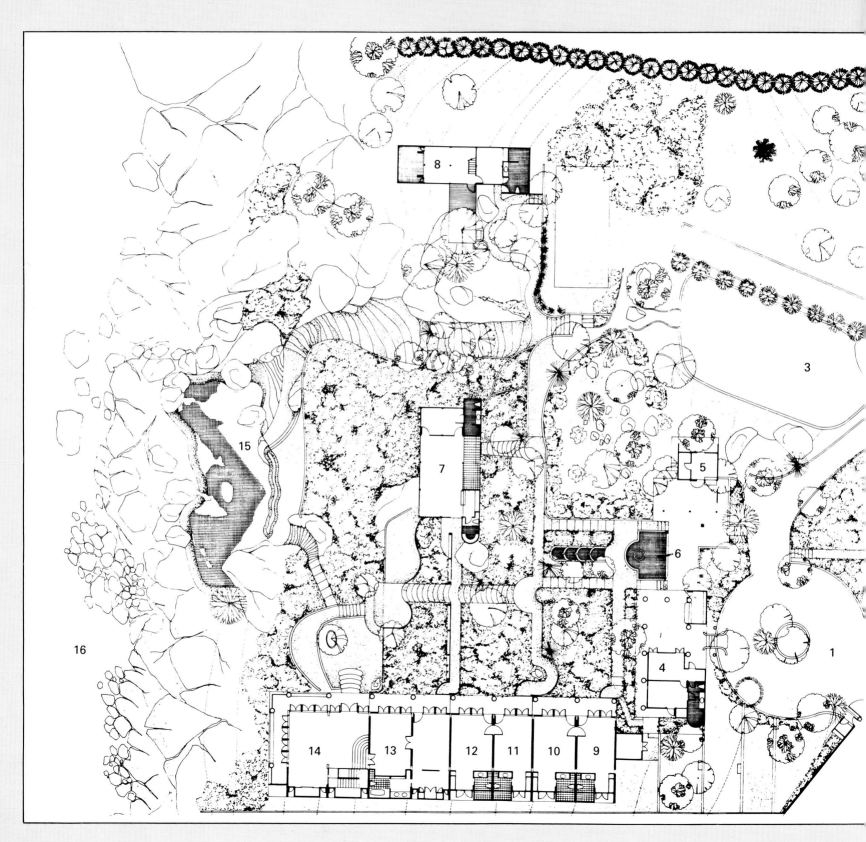

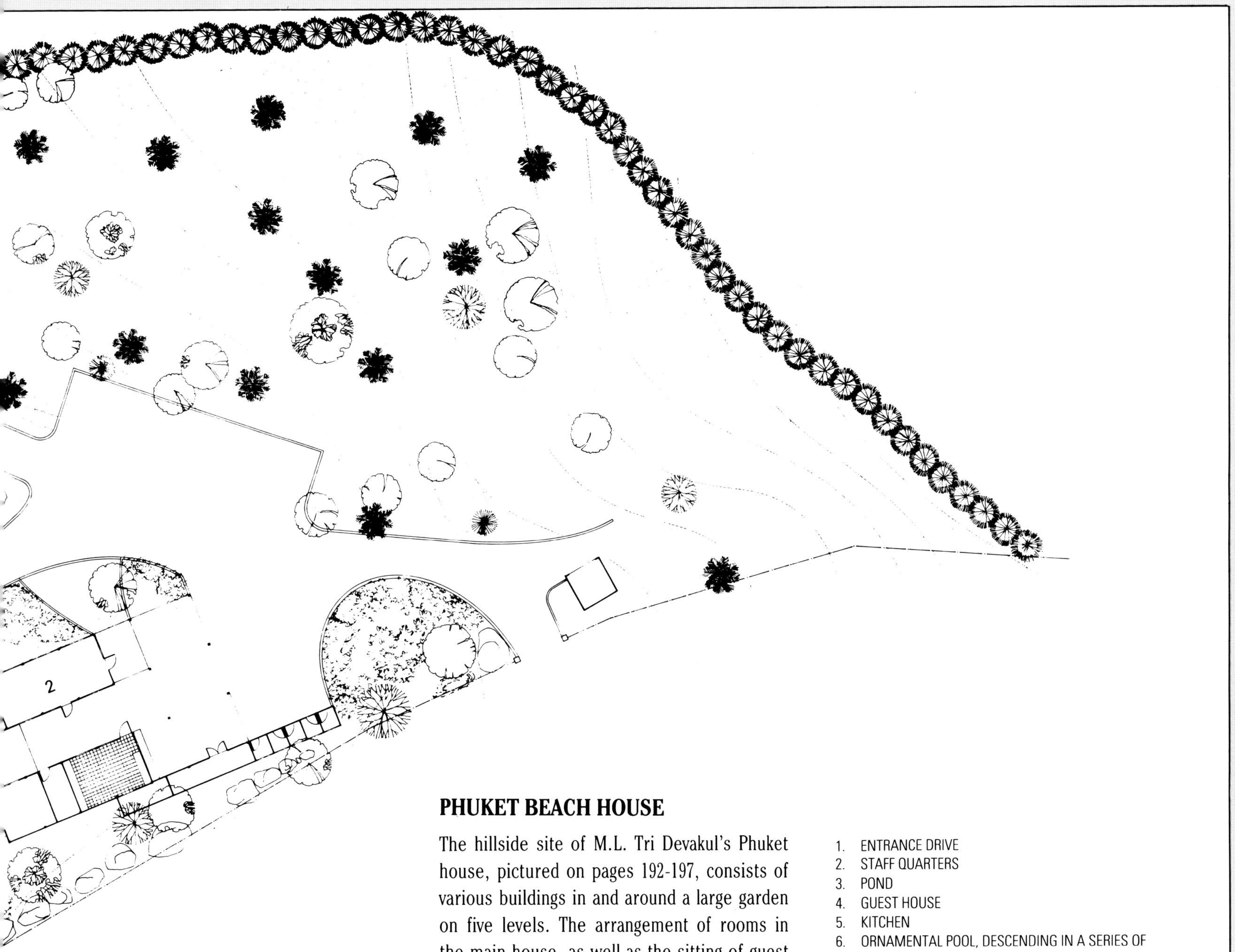

2

PHUKET BEACH HOUSE

The hillside site of M.L. Tri Devakul's Phuket house, pictured on pages 192-197, consists of various buildings in and around a large garden on five levels. The arrangement of rooms in the main house, as well as the sitting of guest houses, ensures maximum privacy and views of the sea. Wherever possible, existing trees were left undisturbed and others were planted to protect the garden from monsoon winds. Steps and pathways connect the different elements of the compound.

1. ENTRANCE DRIVE
2. STAFF QUARTERS
3. POND
4. GUEST HOUSE
5. KITCHEN
6. ORNAMENTAL POOL, DESCENDING IN A SERIES OF LEVELS DOWN THE HILL
7. DINING PAVILION
8. GUEST HOUSE
9.-12. GUEST ROOMS
13. MASTER BEDROOM SUITE
14. LIVING ROOM
15. SALT-WATER SWIMMING POOL
16. ANDAMAN SEA

Side elevation of M.L. Tri's house in Phuket;
the guest rooms are on the top two levels,
while the lowest contains the large living room
overlooking the sea.

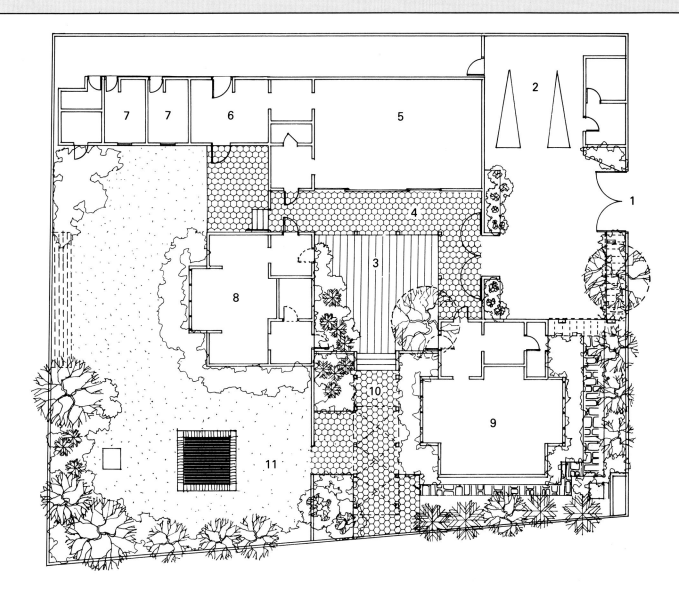

CONTEMPORARY CLUSTER HOUSE

The modern house of Islay Lyons and Manop Charoensuk, pictured on pages 170, 174-175, has three Western-style units around a wooden deck. The large living room forms one side, while two bedroom units are on opposite sides. A large rain tree was retained during construction and provides shade for the deck.

1. ENTRANCE GATE
2. GARAGE
3. CENTRAL DECK
4. COVERED TILED WALKWAY
5. LIVING ROOM
6. KITCHEN
7. SERVANTS' ROOM
8. BEDROOM
9. BEDROOM
10. LATERITE TERRACE
11. GARDEN POOL

INDEX